How to Write and Publish
A Local History Book

Unpacking Memories
Into A Book Construction Zone

A Case Study

Copyright © 2020 Clyde Scheib and Brian Wilde
All Rights Reserved
First Edition
A&EM Publishing
AriselioN
Inquiries: AriselioN@gmail.com
Available on Amazon.com

Back cover: Steampunk Gear Clock 19th century

ISBN: 9798657301281

How to Write and Publish
A Local History Book

Unpacking Memories
Into A Book Construction Zone

A Case Study

Clyde Scheib and Brian Wilde

A Note to the Reader

This case study is a collaboration by Clyde Scheib and Brian Wilde who explain the tools and techniques used in creating a local history book.

Throughout the book Clyde is referred to as the "Author" and Brian is referred to as the "Editor".

Table of Contents

Introduction

Chapter 1. Unpacking Memories • 1

Road Stories • 45

Covered Bridge Lives • 55

Unearthing a Historic Village • 61

Genealogy at the Cemetery • 71

Deliverable • 79

Chapter 2. Book Construction Zone • 81

Chapter 3. Marketing Local History • 103

Leaving Tips • 109

Appendix • 113

Acknowledgments • 117

Introduction: When the Cows Come Home ...

This is a companion book to *West Seven Stars and Beyond: Preserving Local History* by Clyde Scheib and describes how a local history book is researched, written and published. Although concentrated on local history, this approach could be adapted to family history, memoirs and genealogy.

This photo "When the cows come home" . . . (usually led by food) highlights the rural nature of a local history book. This view is of West Seven Stars Road facing northwest from the Kennedy Covered Bridge in East Vincent Township, Chester County, Pennsylvania. The photo caption is from Estelle Cremers who wrote the book *30,000 Acres Vincent and Pikeland Townships from 1686 to 1850.* The Author considers Estelle his mentor. On the right side of the photo is the Kennedy Farm, now the Kimberton Waldorf School. The barn on the left, also part of the Kennedy Farm, burned down in later years.

With the book in hand and the project completed, the Author and Editor laughed once again as we did throughout this whole process and sat back and reflected on how this happened; how two people from different backgrounds recorded a wealth of local history storylines preserved for future generations.

It started with the Editor participating on a task force to create a conceptual plan for a park in a historical village. When asked, the Author stepped up and gave the historical background and significance of Parker Ford Village in both canal transportation and life in the 19th century. The project, called The Parker Ford Historic Park Conceptual Plan is available to the public. This subsequent research became a core chapter and started in motion the storyline process described herein.

Upon reflection, we decided to document the research techniques used in creating the local history book *West Seven Stars and Beyond: Preserving Local History*. History and telling storylines is Author Clyde Scheib's strong suite. The Editor absorbed the stories and alongside the Author, moved content from research to chapters to a published book on Amazon.

This now has become a case study on how to write and publish a local history book. The approach to creating a book of this type is divided into three parts; first, how to write the book; second, how to publish the book; and third, sharing or marketing.

Before we start, introductions are appropriate . . .

The Author

Clyde Scheib

West Seven Stars and Beyond
Preserving Local History

(ISBN: 978-1706215431) 315 pages
Publish date: November 27, 2019 (B&W)
February 18, 2020 (Color)

Clyde and Alda Scheib at the Kurtland Dairy Farm "Breakfast on the Farm" event near Elverson PA.

Published book on Amazon.com

This is Clyde and Alda Scheib, the photo taken in front of the Kurtland dairy farm near Elverson PA during a Breakfast on the Farm event ("Choose PA Dairy"). Pennsylvania ranks second in the nation for the number of dairy farms and 99 percent of the states farms being family owned. Clyde and Alda were dairy farmers for much of their career in Chester County.

As mentioned, Clyde Scheib is the author of the *West Seven Stars and Beyond: Preserving Local History* which was created in late 2019. We are fortunate Clyde took great care in understanding the local history around him over an 80 year period.

We hope to share with you how the book was created and published and got into the Author's hands. Also, how others can replicate the process to create their own local history book.

The Editor

Brian Wilde

West Seven Stars and Beyond
Preserving Local History

Editor and Publisher

Book that Clyde read that gave him idea to preserve local history.

Editor at ancestral home in German outpost village in region previously known as Galicia.

As the Editor and Publisher of *West Seven Stars and Beyond*, the goal was to preserve local history, in an easily readable and photo centric manner. The medium chosen was a book on Amazon.com. By using Print on Demand (POD) technology, the Author and Editor were taken out of the book distribution loop and at the same time, made the book accessible to family, friends and the community.

In the above photo, the Editor is standing in front of the family house in his ancestral village which was a German outpost in the Austrian Hungarian Empire, near the modern day L'viv, Ukraine. This is highlighted in the book, *Wilde Genealogy, European and Canadian Heritage 1800-1945* by Kathleen Wilde. This genealogy book, created by the Editor and his aunt was shared with Clyde and he got the idea to create a local history book along these same lines.

We hope to show you how Clyde's concept of a local history book came to fruition.

The Goal: Preserve Local History

Build Storyline
- Create new content
- Review author's notes, storylines and oral histories of the period
- Conduct additional research
- Address genealogy
- Enhance storylines with visuals; maps, photos, charts
- Strategize approach; limit to nearby landmarks

Goal
- To preserve local history
- Publish a history book using KDP
- Place on Amazon.com
- Share with community; family, friends and local residents

Priscilla Murray Brownback, Levi Brownback holding Gladys Swinehart (Clyde Scheib's mother)

Amazon Kindle Direct Publishing (KDP)

Our goal was to create a local history storyline including a segment on family genealogy.

The Editor's role is to understand the Author's reference materials and notes and to fill in gaps by conducting research. Both Editor and Author worked closely on the books content.

The personal history storylines are enhanced with visuals to make the book interesting and readable. One core guideline: historical content had to be in close proximity to the Author's residence.

Genealogy is a close cousin to local history. Genealogy is about family member relationships with other family members; whereas local history is about people's storyline and involvement in a landmark or event. One crossover, in genealogy and local history, is a persons birth, baptism, marriage and death. As required, the Editor resolves genealogy brick walls or research roadblocks. These breakthroughs are described in the "Scheib Genealogy" chapter of the book.

Author / Editor Roles
Two Operating Scenarios

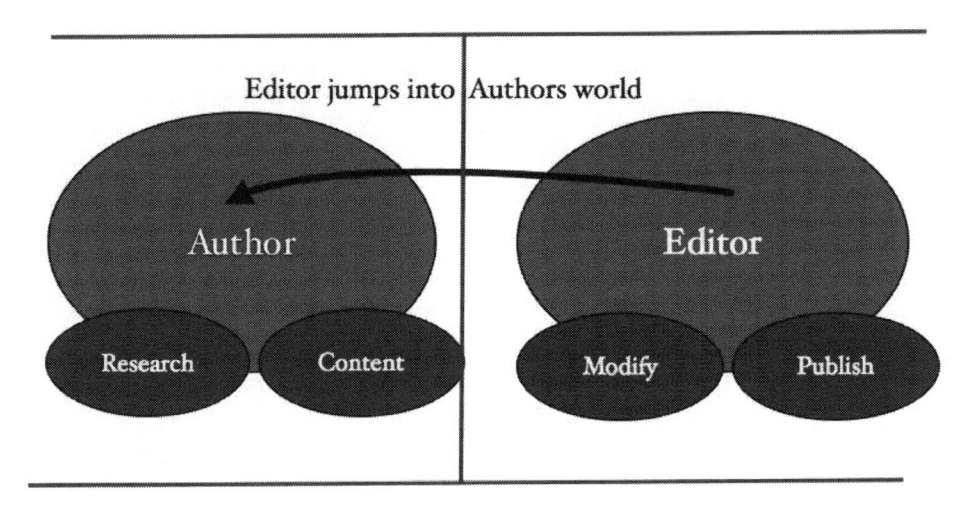

Editor jumps into Authors world

Author | Editor

Research | Content | Modify | Publish

Alternate scenario: Author jumps into Editors world (not shown)

There are two operating scenarios in creating a book. The first is the Editor enters into the Author's world and assists in developing content acceptable to the Author. This method requires close collaboration of ideas and numerous intermittent reviews with the Author. This is called a Development Editor approach and was used in this case study.

The second operating scenario is the Author enters into the Editor's world and presents a manuscript for review and input. Once approved, the publishing mechanics begin. In some cases, the Author takes the lead in self publishing the book.

Although an Author may have the skill set to jump into the editors world, he/she may choose not to do so, preferring to stay in a writing role and instead engage an Editor to publish and bring the book to market.

> People are trapped in history and history is trapped in them.
>
> - James Baldwin

> An author is somebody who writes a story. It doesn't matter if you're a kid or if you're a grown-up, it doesn't matter if the book gets published and lots of people get to read it, or if you make just one copy and you share that book with one friend.
>
> - Jarrett J. Krosoczka

> To live in hearts we leave behind, is not to die.
>
> - Thomas Campbell

Chapter 1. Unpacking Memories

> An editor, at most, releases energy. - Maxwell Perkins

The Author and Editor, collaborating closely, begin the process of creating the local history content. This is the Authors first published book.

Create Local History Content

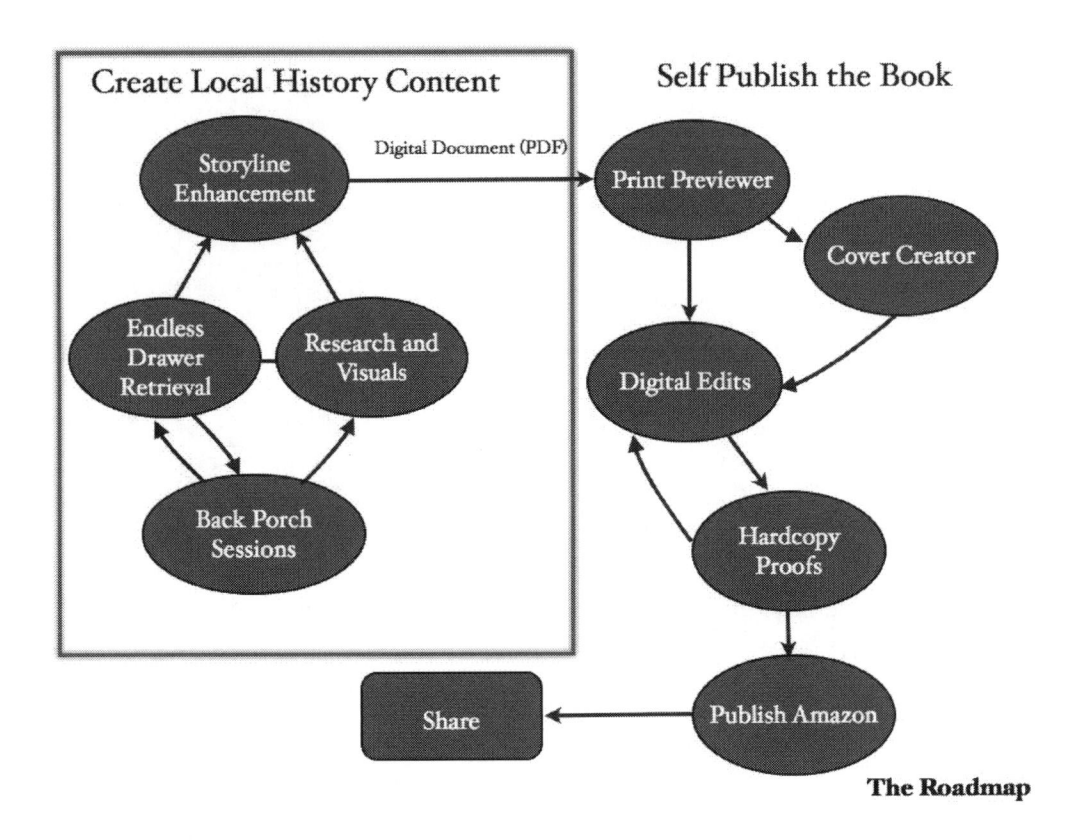

The Roadmap

The Roadmap: Create Local History Content
This is a roadmap for writing, editing and publishing a book. There are three parts; 1) Create Local History Content, 2) Self Publish the Book and 3) Share.

In Creating Local History Content, one of the first steps is to gather all of the Author's research to date; including newsletters, articles, oral histories, local historical books and historical photos in the Author's possession. This is augmented by current day photos taken by the Editor. This review was done in what became known as the Back Porch Sessions, a term we used in jest, but was an actual physical place where the Author and Editor met on a regular basis.

Once the current baseline of information was available, new research began. Note, that gathering of materials is by topic being discussed or under review, which would narrow the research only to that topic. This keeps the writing manageable and focused. As more topics are discussed, the remainder of the Author's knowledge and mounds of materials surfaced. In this project, this was called the Endless Drawer Retrieval, a pun with an element of humor, yet an effective way that materials surfaces from somewhere in the Author's house, on an iterative, by topic basis.

Research is the backbone of any local history book and can be extensive and time consuming, yet gratifying. Many history stories have been told and retold many times over the decades. The Author places his perspective from a position of knowledge and local expertise. For example, we all know about one room schoolhouses, they have been written about in the past as to how class was taught and the contents of the building. But having the Author describe experiences from actually attending a one room schoolhouse, adds value for the readers.

Research can include trips to the local historical societies in the region, in this case the Chester County Historical Society (CCHS) in West Chester, Pennsylvania. Resources in this county library include vintage maps, newspaper clippings, family genealogy stories, books and periodicals at the township and county level and an extensive historical photo collection. The newspaper clippings covers 1810-1970 and are divided by family surname, county and township. The library also includes an extensive collection of books and letters of Chester County's own literary critic, international traveller and poet; the great Bayard Taylor (1825-1878).

Walking tours of areas under investigation became important research aids for the Editor and Author. The resulting photo documentation of taverns, grist mills, canals, waterways and historic houses can be compared to past historical village walking tours.

Here are some of the research sources used:
1. Landmark's view of it's own history
2. Walking tour pamphlets
3. Local cemetery tour
4. "Find a Grave" website
5. Ancestry.com website

6. National Register of Historic Places
7. Historical society Facebook pages and blogs
8. Historical books like, *The History of the Underground Railroad by Robert Smedley* (1883); and the informative *History of Chester County by Furthey and Cope* (1881)
9. Living Places Neighborhoods website
10. Master plans or conceptual studies created by consultants looking to preserve history

Creating local history content uses a Storyline Enhancement methodology. This incorporates charts, vintage photos, new photos; all applied to the text of the manuscript. A storyline is a base story from the Author's viewpoint with visuals from research efforts to enrich the story. Other visual aides are: family trees, genealogy lineage charts, maps, handwritten letters, newspaper clippings and birth and death records. A general rule is to have a photo on each page in the book that augments the storyline to keep the content fresh and easy to read.

As research materials amassed, the Editor placed resulting content in the Apple Pages word processing program, which is best for a photo laden book. Pages is easier to position photos on a page layout than say, Microsoft's Word. Also, the conversion into a PDF format is more streamlined and takes less steps. Yet, Microsoft Word can be used to create content, if desired, although more cumbersome. More on this topic later.

This case study is not a guide for multiple genres, like fiction tales, nor an analysis as to why an author would self publish versus traditional publish. The Editor choose to self publish the book for expediency and full control of the end product.

Content Creation Phase
Time Management

The Back Porch Sessions
- meet same day and time each week
- plan for long run; typical takes months to complete a draft book
- requires stamina to complete a book
- engage editor early in process

Quality vs Time
- use fastest creation method (i.e. taking photos of photos) within acceptable quality range
- not a precise process
- conduct ongoing edits
- track sources

The Back Porch

> People generally don't recognize how long it takes to conceive, publish, and write a book. - Neil deGrasse Tyson

Create Local History Content: Time Management
As mentioned, the Back Porch Sessions was actually a back porch where the Author and Editor met on a regular basis, used figuratively in this case, as it could be any meeting place. The important point is the sessions are held regularly on a given date and time. The process of creating local history is more a marathon than a sprint and agreeing to a mutually acceptable time to meet eliminates a lot of back and forth phone calls and checking calendars and scheduling around other events or meetings. The Back Porch Sessions are given high priority to move the project forward.

Creating Local History Content
Project Beginnings

"Back Porch" Sessions
- Idea creation / Strategy
- Hand written notes
- Oral history review
- Newspaper accounts
- Vintage photos
- Articles
- Maps
- Books

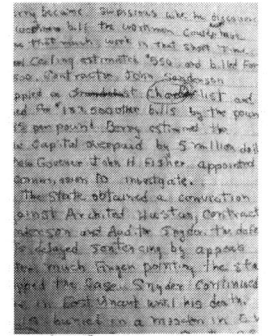

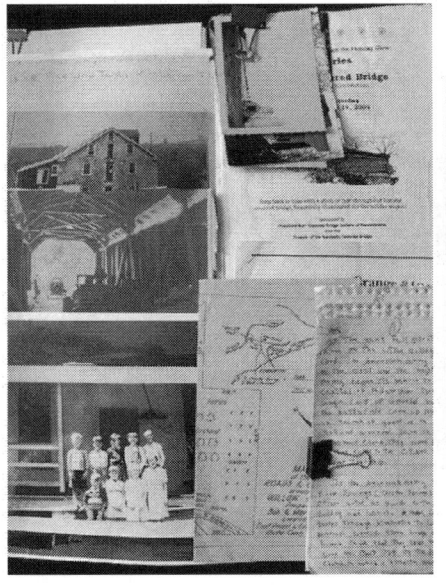

Author notes

Materials in Back Porch Sessions

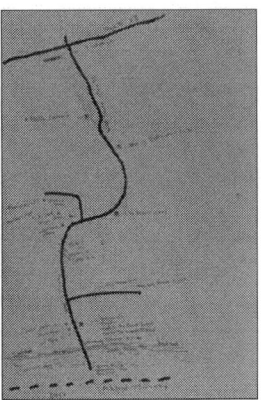

Author drawn map

Create Local History Content: Project Beginnings
The Author's writings are collected and baselined by topic on a rolling weekly schedule. Research materials, both new and existing are either collected on site or taken from the Internet. New storylines are created by the Author, in this case, hand written in a composition book, but for others, it could be typed on a computer.

Over an eighty year period, the Author kept scrupulous handwritten notes, charts and even hand drawn maps related to local history. His sources were his family, organizations he belonged, books and oral histories.

As the Author always said, "History isn't always fresh, it has been written before, just different slants based on the same historical facts." Clyde bolstered his stories by going to source documents, many from the 1800's.

So it would have been easy to transcribe the notes, add the articles and photos and bind it up at Staples. But that's not what we did.

Preserving Local History
"All Around Me" History Approach

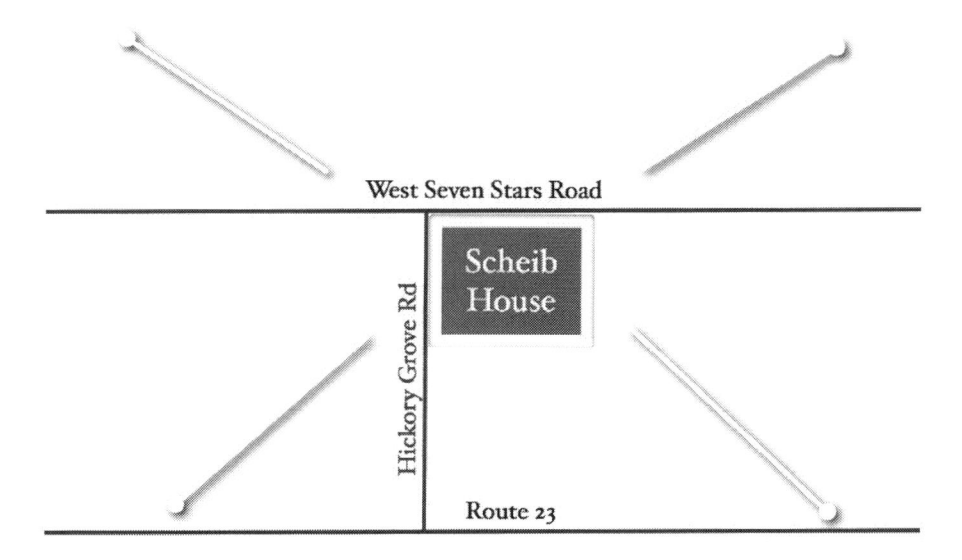

[Diagram: Scheib House at intersection of West Seven Stars Road and Hickory Grove Rd, near Route 23, with arrows radiating outward in four diagonal directions]

Create Local History Content: Preserving Local History
The Author defined a core element of his "all around me" local history approach as the road he had lived on most of his life; West Seven Stars Road. It took the Editor some time to digest this approach, that a road was central to his history storyline. After discovering several early photos of this road and landmarks along the road with a rich history; the dirt road with cows "coming home" began to make sense.

The landmarks on this road include a private school, a yogurt farm, and a covered bridge, which will be described later. Expansion of the "all around me" approach reveals a one room schoolhouse within walking distance of the Author's house, a tavern from a 19th century village and a railroad (Sowbelly) that can be seen from the Author's living room.

This was the unique approach to preserving local history; landmarks and memories within a close proximity to the Author's residence, without regard to township borders or county lines.

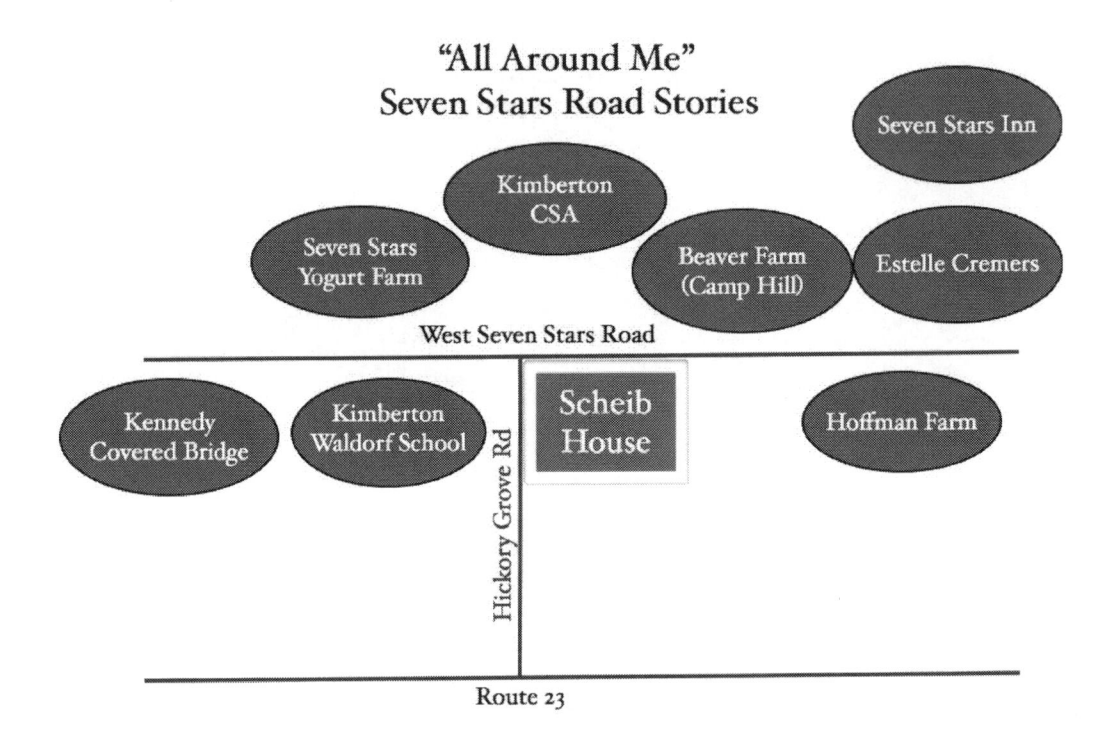

"All Around Me" Seven Stars Road Stories

[Diagram showing landmarks arranged around the Scheib House (Author's House) at the intersection of West Seven Stars Road and Hickory Grove Rd, near Route 23. North of West Seven Stars Road: Seven Stars Yogurt Farm, Kimberton CSA, Beaver Farm (Camp Hill), Estelle Cremers, Seven Stars Inn. South of West Seven Stars Road: Kennedy Covered Bridge, Kimberton Waldorf School, Scheib House, Hoffman Farm.]

Create Local History Content: "All Around Me" Book Structure
The "all around me" local history approach drove the entire book structure. As mentioned, the core of the book is based on the road in front of the Author's house which became Chapter 2, "West on Seven Stars" a reference to West Seven Stars Road in East Vincent Township, Chester County, Pennsylvania. The landmarks on this road are:

- Kennedy Covered Bridge
- Kimberton Waldorf School
- Seven Stars Yogurt Farm
- Kimberton CSA
- Author's House
- Beaver Farm / Camp Hill Transitional Program
- Historian Estelle Cremers Farm
- Kimberton Hunt Subdivision / Hoffman Farm
- Seven Stars Historical Inn

"All Around Me" Full Book Structure

Diagram showing landmarks arranged geographically:

North of West Seven Stars Road: History of Kimberton, Underground Railroad, Seven Stars Yogurt Farm, Sowbelly Railroad, Beaver Farm (Camp Hill), Seven Stars Inn, Estelle Cremers

South of West Seven Stars Road (along Hickory Grove Rd and Route 23): Kennedy Covered Bridge, Kimberton Waldorf School, Scheib House, Farming Life, Unknown Soldiers, One Room Schoolhouse, Genealogy, Bonnie Brae Park, Parker Ford

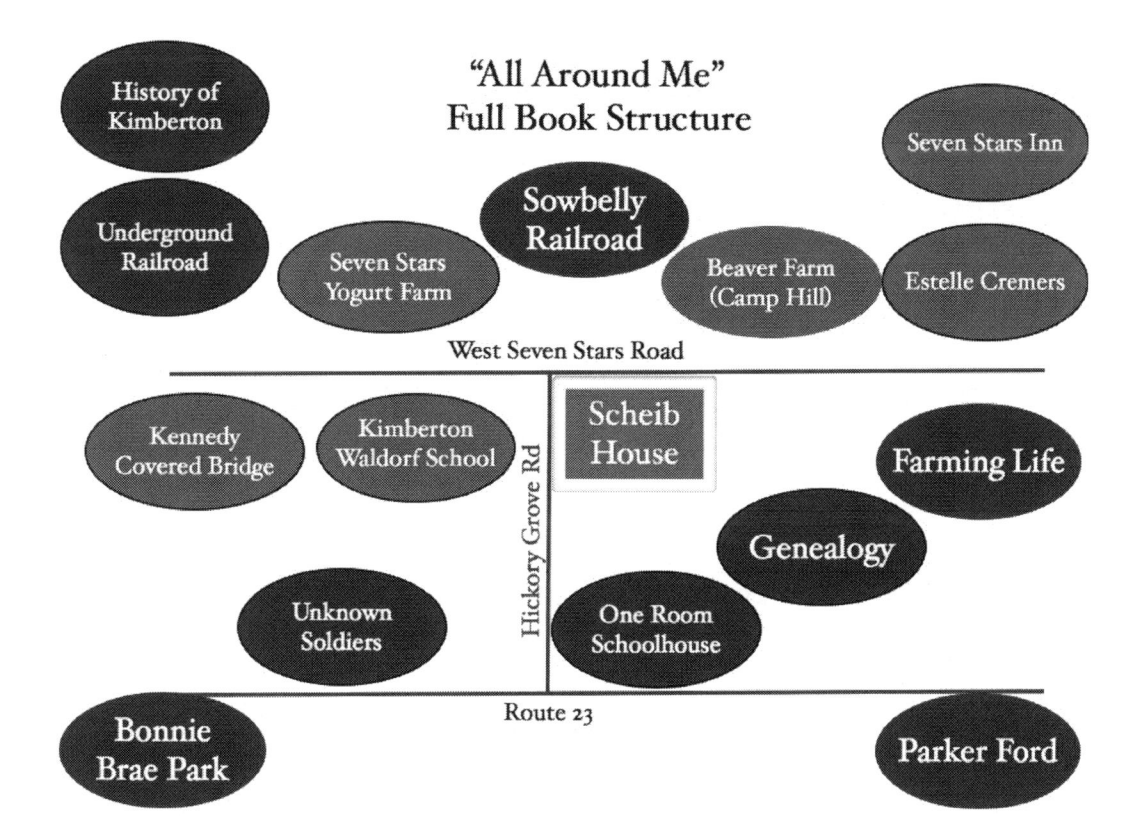

Create Local History Content : "All Around Me" Full Book Structure

The "all around me" local history approach then expanded to landmarks which became chapters in the book:

- "History of Kimberton" (Ch. 1) - one mile from Author's house
- "West on Seven Stars" (Ch 2) - core of book (light color)
- "Parker Ford Village" (Ch. 3) - two miles from Author house
- "Living with Sowbelly" (Ch. 4) - can see from front window
- "My One Room Schoolhouse" (Ch. 5) - short walk
- "Underground Railroad" (Ch. 6) - one mile from Author's house
- "Bonnie Brae Park" (Ch. 7) - two miles from Author's house
- "Scheib Genealogy" (Ch. 8) - in Author house
- "Farming Life" (Ch. 9) - field next door
- "Two Forgotten Names" (Ch. 10) - one mile from house
- "Unknown Soldiers" (Ch. 11) - one/half mile from house

Content Creation Phase
Editor Tools

Apple "Pages" word processing
Grab - MacOS selective screen capture
iPhone for photos, document sharing
Apple Mac computer

Pic Monkey - image editor
Scanner for text creation
Adobe Acrobat - photo enhancer
Alternative: Microsoft "Word" word processing

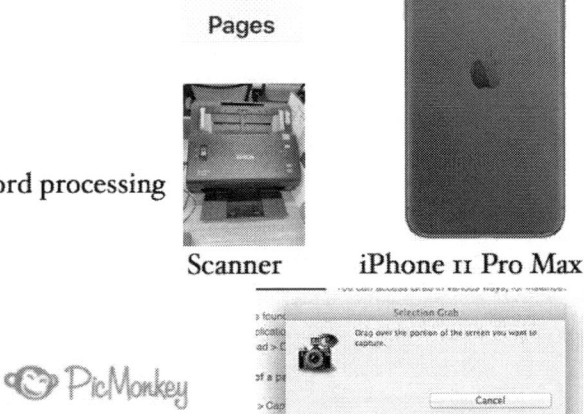

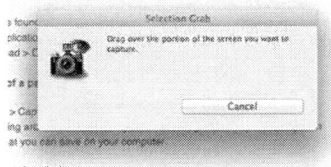

Pages

Scanner

iPhone 11 Pro Max

Editor workstation

Screen Grab

Content Creation Phase: Editor Tools
Key self publishing tools used by the Editor (excluding Amazon Kindle Direct Publishing (KDP) vendor tools) follow.

Apple's Word Processing Program "Pages" is best applied when graphics and images are intermingled with text. Pages can be used from the start of the book to the finished print-ready PDF. Also, Pages has a good export feature to other formats. Microsoft Word, on the other hand, requires another application, like Adobe Acrobat, to complete the start to finish print-ready PDF.

Grab is a simple MacOS tool for selective screen capture. An example is capturing an image from one source, like an Internet photo and placing it in the working document. This becomes one of the most used tools and saved extensive amounts of time with placing photos in a document. iPhone 11 pro Max is the smartphone used to capture photos. It should be noted, that for every photo used in the book, there were five to ten photos actually taken. The photos are stored in a computer folder, in this case a MacBook Pro, compatible with the Pages word processing program. Note, a Windows computer can also be used but can be more time consuming dealing with a large number of photos.

Pic Monkey is an on-line image editor for cover photos and key images.

An in-line scanner to convert hard copy physical text to digital text was used from the Tech Center at the main County Library.

Adobe Acrobat is used to enhance key photos.

Storyline Enhancement Techniques

#1 Creative Writing
#2 The Village Walking Tour
#3 Converting Oral Histories
#4 Historical Author Accounts
#5 Historical Paintings
#6 Notes, Yearbooks, Newsletters
#7 Genealogy: The Lineage Chart
#8 Genealogy: The Ancestry Website
#9 Genealogy: "Find a Grave" Website
#10 Genealogy: Cemetery Tour
#11 Engaging a Genealogy Consultant*
#12 The Wedding Attendees*
#13 The Shared Voyage Account*
#14 Sharing Knowledge from a Consultant*
#15 Historical Newspapers
#16 Converting Author Interviews
#17 Vintage Photos
#18 Additional Storyline Enhancement Techniques

* separate case study

Create Local History Content: Storyline Enhancement Techniques
The following is an overview of the techniques for creating content:

#1 Creative Writing for new content. In this case study, the Author used hand written notes of local narratives.

#2 The Village Walking Tour consisted of two types; a previously conducted walking tour, with a pamphlet guide showing the route and landmark descriptions; and a current period tour conducted taking photos of existing landmarks, creating hand drawn route maps and explaining each landmark.

#3 Converting Oral Histories into readable text.

#4 Historical Author accounts with portrait drawings of historical figures.

#5 Historical Paintings to augment storyline including Author's father portrait painting, revolutionary war paintings and other local paintings.

#6 Notes, Yearbooks and Newsletters used to initiate storylines.

#7 Genealogy: The Lineage Chart shows relationships of ancestors.

#8 Genealogy: The Ancestry.com website confirmed ancestor relationships, and dates for birthday, marriage, children and death.

#9 Genealogy: "Find a Grave" website shows ancestor burial with tombstone photo.

#10 Genealogy: Cemetery Tour of several local cemeteries to discover actual grave sites of the family.

#11 Engaging a Genealogy Consultant to find ancestors and their daily life in an ancestral village.

#12 The Wedding Attendees recounts the wedding service, priest, best man, family attendees and children set in an ancestral village.

#13 The Shared Voyage Account is a storyline from an ocean crossing voyage trip from a port (like Hamburg, Germany) to North America (like Philadelphia or Montreal).

#14 Sharing Knowledge from a Consultant is documenting email communiques from a consultants response to questions explaining diverse and complicated genealogy or history topics. These are later embedded into the storyline for additional color commentary.

#15 Historical Newspapers provide news accounts of events, whether a disastrous event like a covered bridge fire, to attendees at a mid 19th century birthday party.

#16 Converting Author Interviews, by transcribing an oral history recording or converting an interview into readable storyline text.

#17 Vintage Photos in a local history book are important additions, either from early postcard photos or vintage family camera photos. Photos can include:
- Transportation; horse and buggy, canal, trains, roads, covered bridges
- Schoolhouses; residence houses, farms, taverns, churches
- People; portraits, group photos
- Events; marriage, death, covered bridge anniversary, Independence Day

#18 Additional Storyline Enhancement Techniques is a summary of additional techniques used on the *West Seven Stars and Beyond* case study.

Next we explore details and examples of each of the Storyline Enhancement Techniques mentioned previously.

Storyline Enhancement Technique
#1 Creative Writing

Creative Writing
- Verbally discuss storylines
- Author creates storyline content
- Both Author and Editor conduct additional research
  - Author researches personal files
  - Internet research by Editor
  - Chester County Historical Society
- Locate visuals, vintage photos
- Photos to enrich storylines
- Create maps, charts
- Make content informative and readable
- Editor creates drafts of text with photos

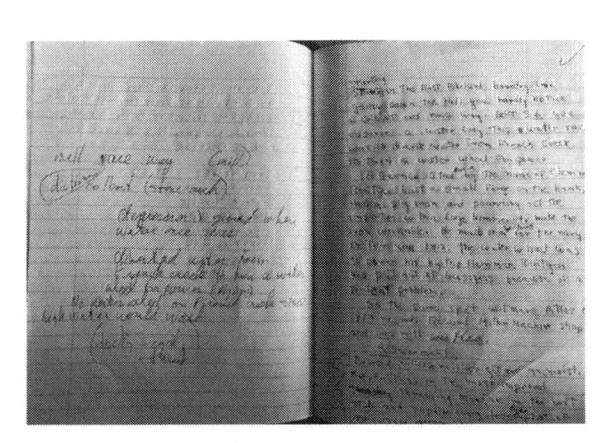

Author's composition book

"When I write a book, I write a book for myself; the reaction is up to the reader. It's not my business whether people like or dislike it" - Paulo Coelho

Storyline Enhancement Technique #1: Creative Writing
In this case study, the Author utilized hand written text in a composition book following an outline. The Editor's role is to take whatever the Author creates and make it presentable with photos and pertinent research.

UNPACKING MEMORIES

Storyline Enhancement Technique
#2 The Village Walking Tour of Yesterday

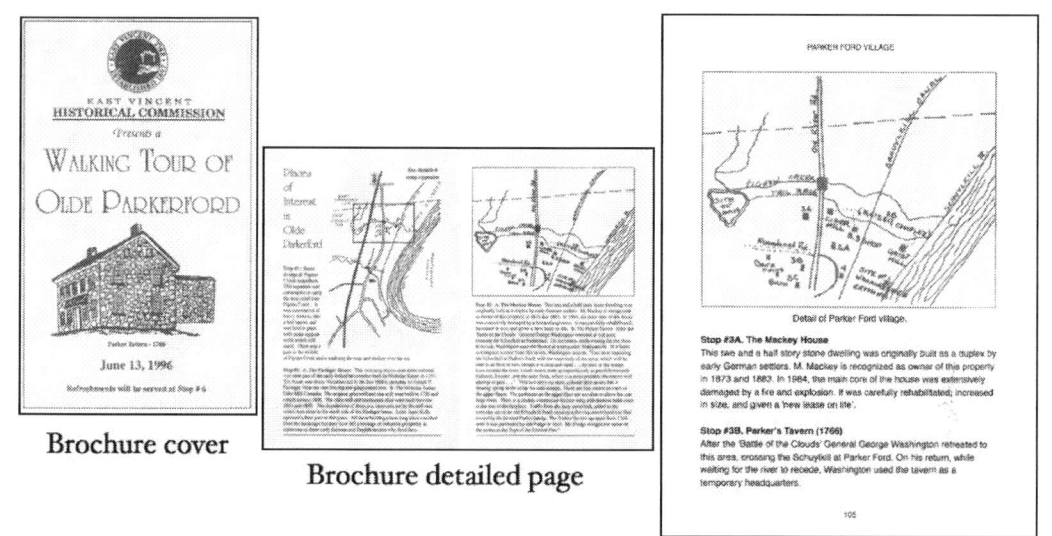

Brochure cover

Brochure detailed page

Result: brochure sketch with modified content

Storyline Enhancement Technique #2: The Village Walking Tour of Yesterday

A brochure of a walking tour of "Old Parkerford", conducted over thirty years ago (1996), was uncovered by the Author. A map with details of each stop was enlarged and included in the book *West Seven Stars and Beyond*. Vintage photos of the tour stops were researched and added to this content.

An Example:
Stop #3B. The Parker Tavern (1766)
After the 'Battle of the Clouds' General George Washington retreated to this area, crossing the Schuylkill at Parkerford. While waiting for the river to recede, Washington used the Tavern as a temporary headquarters.

Storyline Enhancement Technique #2 The Village Walking Tour of Today (cont'd)

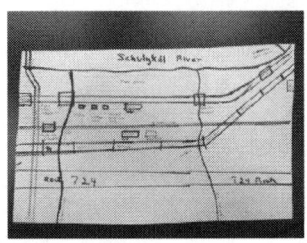

Parker Ford Village Area Map by Author

List of Photos

Top: Photo 4 Parkers House
Bottom: Photo 5 Parkers House with steps to canal

Storyline Enhancement Technique #2 (cont'd): The Village Walking Tour of Today

Here the Author and Editor are making an actual walking tour of Parker Ford Village landmarks. Together we made 24 stops taking digital photos of historic landmarks using an iPhone. This was compared to the 1996 Walking Tour and incorporated into the chapter. The Author subsequently created a map of the Village. The photos were shared with team members participating in the Parker Ford Historic Park Conceptual Plan.

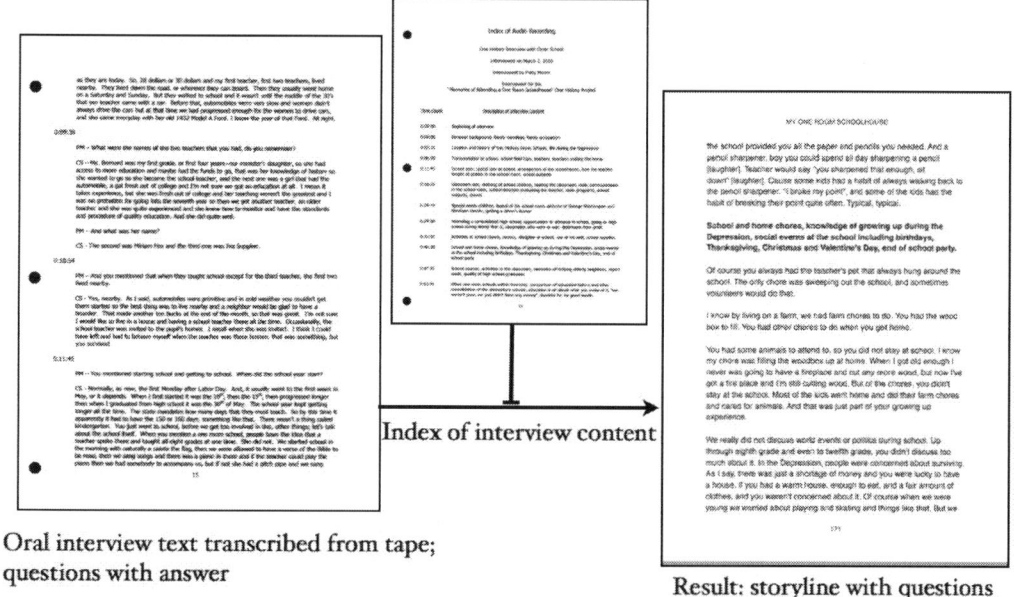

Storyline Enhancement Technique #3 Converting Oral Histories

Oral interview text transcribed from tape; questions with answer

Index of interview content

Result: storyline with questions eliminated

Storyline Enhancement Technique #3: Converting Oral Histories
There were several oral histories reviewed. A half dozen snippets by various local residents were selected based on relevance to content in the book and were placed in the Appendix.

One oral history stood out. That oral history was a project from Bucks County Community College Historic Preservation Program, *Memories of Attending a One Room Schoolhouse* conducted by Patty Moore Meter interviewing the Author.

Shown (left) are a sampling of questions by the interviewer (Ms. Meter) and the verbal response by the Author. The question was subsequently eliminated and built into the Author's response.

In the center is the index of the audio recording with the time count and the "Description of the Interview Content". This description became the heading and guided where to insert the Author's content or response. The result is shown (right).

Storyline Enhancement Technique #4 Historical Author Accounts (1883 Dr. Robert Smedley)

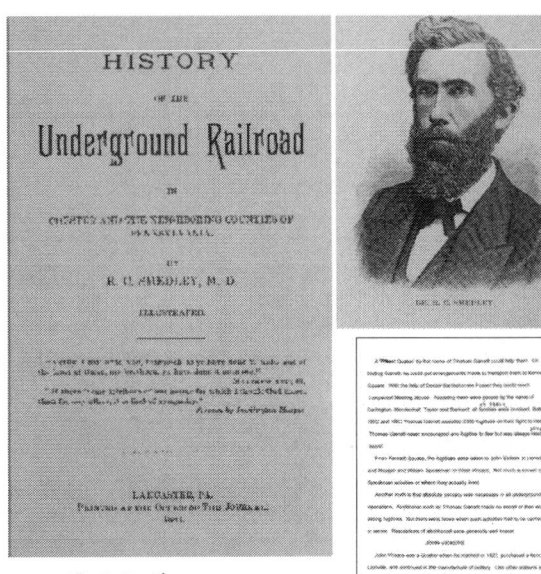

Original resource

Author base content

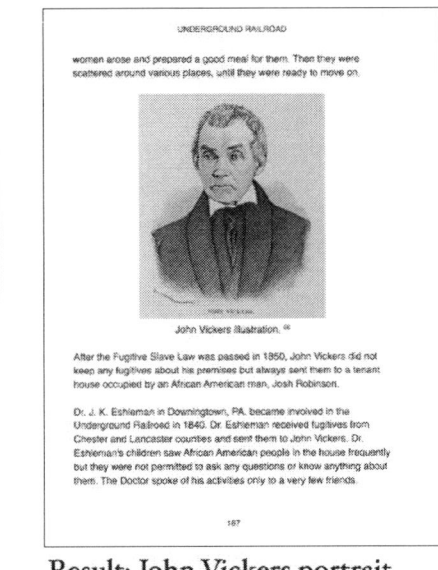

Result: John Vickers portrait with storyline

Storyline Enhancement Technique #4: Historical Author Accounts (1883 Dr. Robert Smedley)

The historical author account provided real life paintings that augmented the Author's content. The book, *History of the Underground Railroad in Chester County* by R.C. Smedley M.D. (1883) West Chester, PA provided portrait illustrations of key figures in the local area. On the left is the inside page book title, in the center is Dr. Smedley and the Author's draft account. A result of this research is the John Vickers portrait from the Smedley book and the description that became part of Chapter 6, "The Underground Railroad".

Storyline Enhancement Technique #4 (cont'd) Historical Author Accounts (Graceanna Lewis)

Underground Railroad in Chester County

Graceanna Lewis marker in Kimberton, Pennsylvania

Storyline Enhancement Technique #4: (cont'd) Historical Author Accounts (Grace Anne Lewis)
A second example includes the portrait of GraceAnne Lewis from the Smedley book, *History of the Underground Railroad in Chester County*. It is coupled with the current GraceAnne Lewis marker in Kimberton, Pennsylvania near her families farm. The marker describes her life as a botanist and Underground Railroad leader in the local area.

Storyline Enhancement Technique #5 Historical Paintings

Storyline Enhancement Technique #5: Historical Paintings
Historical paintings often add legitimacy and expertise in describing local history. Paintings are used when vintage photos are not available or practical, due to the time period before cameras. Paintings give another perspective to being there. Here is a sampling of different types of historical paintings used in this case study (clockwise upper left):

- Painting by Dorothy Weikel of cave where French Canadian trapper Bezzilian lived near Spring City PA.
- The village of Kimberton circa 1835 by John Pierce.
- The Author's father, Walter Scheib, in a painting on a wall in the Author's dining room. An iPhone photo of the Scheib family painting was digitally captured and added to the book.
- Residence of John Vickers from the *History of the Underground Railroad in Chester County, PA* by R.C. Smedley MD 1883.
- Painting by Xavier della Gatta (1782) of the British Light Infantry and Light Dragoons attacking the Pennsylvania camp on September 20, 1777.

- Fugitive slaves undercover, from *History of the Underground Railroad in Chester County PA* by R.C. Smedley MD 1883.
- Washington and Lafayette at Valley Forge circa 1778 by John Ward Dunsmore 1907.

Storyline Enhancement Technique #6 Notes, Yearbooks and Newsletters

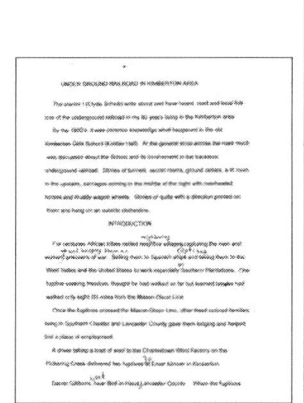

Notes on Kimberton Village talk

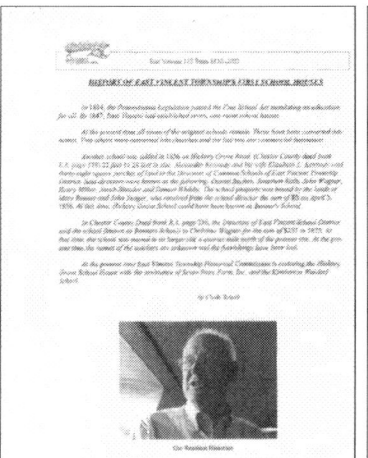

Township Yearbook article; *East Vincent 175 Years 1832-2007*

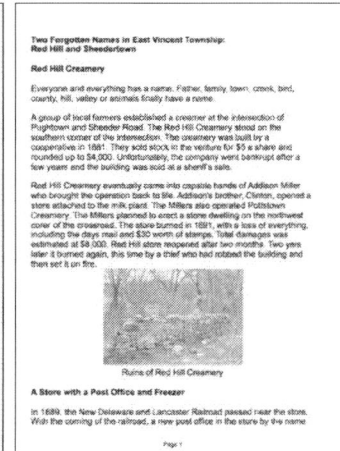

Township newsletters

Storyline Enhancement Technique #6: Notes, Yearbooks and Newsletters

The Author's many years as a public figure in the historical community gave rise to talks about the history around him. Several notes from these talks were recovered and became a baseline for creating content.

East Vincent Township (Chester County, PA) celebrated its 175th anniversary in the community (1832-2007) with a Township Yearbook. Several local history articles supplied by the Author were retrieved to create content.

The Township also publishes a quarterly Newsletter and typically includes articles of interest from the Historical Commission. Several articles from the Author over a 50 year span were collected to create book content.

Storyline Enhancement Technique #7 Genealogy: The Lineage Chart

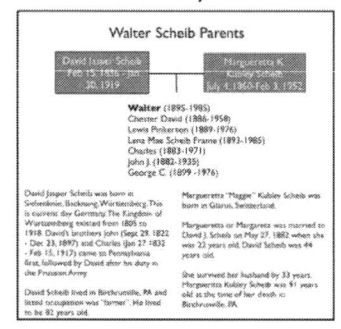

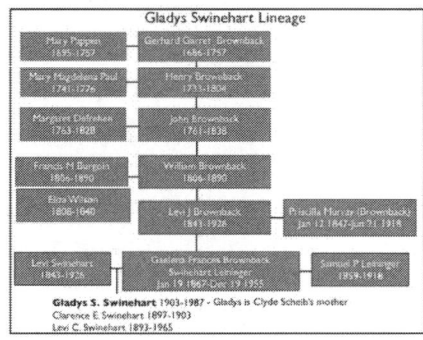

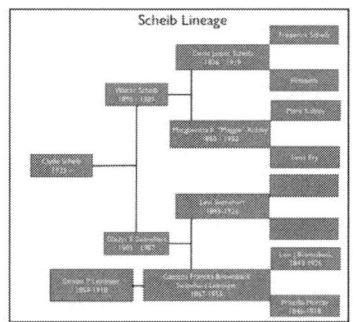

Storyline Enhancement Technique #7: Genealogy / The Lineage Chart

This Storyline Enhancement Technique compiles family history records, cemetery data and parish life records into a higher level family tree called The Lineage Chart. This allows the Editor and Author to organize and understand family relationships and share with the general readership.

The "Walter Scheib Parents" lineage chart shows the Author's grandparents and their children. Recording who passed away first, leaves by calculation, the number of years the spouse was a widow.

The family photo shown in "The Scheib Brownback Swinehart Connection" is Clyde Scheib's mother as a child. This rare photo was discovered on the Ancestry.com website.

Note, the blank position holders in the "Scheib Lineage" allow future family historians to continue the genealogy research.

Storyline Enhancement Technique #8 Genealogy: The Ancestry.com Website

David Scheib family tree (Ancestry.com)

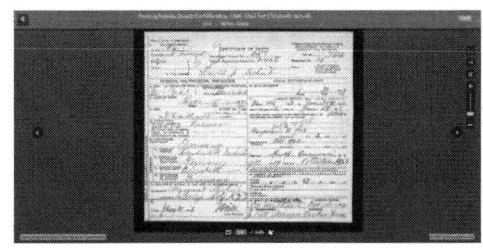

David Scheib Certificate of Death showing parents name (Ancestry.com)

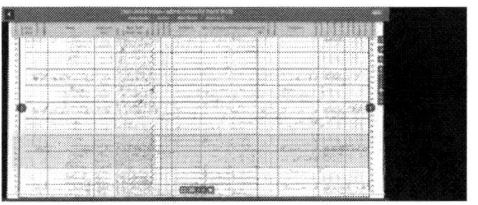

1910 Census (Ancestry.com)

Storyline Enhancement Technique #8: Genealogy / The Ancestry.com Website

One of the foremost genealogy sites, Ancestry or Ancestry.com is fully accessible at the County Public Library. From the website, David Scheib's Certificate of Death in West Vincent Township, Chester County, PA shows his birthplace as Germany and parents as Fredrick and Elizabeth. This resolved a family brick wall (roadblock) as to the parents name.

Several family trees on the Ancestry.com website appeared accurate, although several pieces of data were unverified. The census data from 1910 is informative.

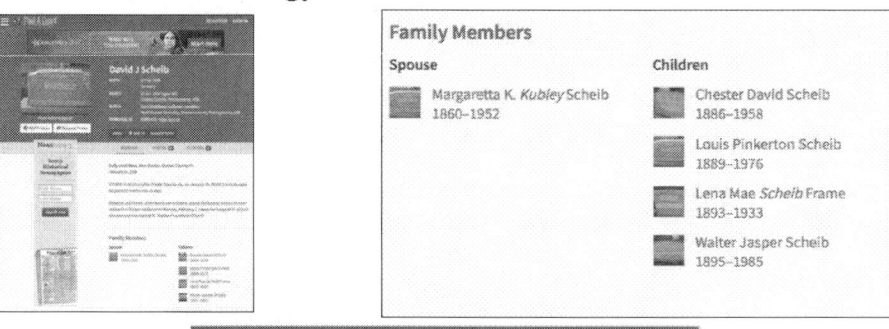

Storyline Enhancement Technique #9 Genealogy: The "Find a Grave" Website

Find a Grave site for David J. Scheib with detail

Storyline Enhancement Technique #9: Genealogy / The "Find a Grave" Website

Independent of Ancestry.com, is the "Find A Grave" website, specializing in cemetery tombstone photos and family tree data submitted by volunteer members. Some family tree data can be deduced from the tombstone information, in this case, David and Margaret Scheib's children.

Storyline Enhancement Technique
#10 Genealogy: Cemetery Tour

Storyline Enhancement Technique #10: Genealogy / Cemetery Tour
The actual cemeteries, in this case, St. Matthews Luthern Cemetery in West Vincent Township, Chester County, PA provides a wealth of genealogy information that complements the "Find A Grave" website.

The Author and Editor toured the local cemeteries and recorded, using photos, for inclusion in the "Scheib Genealogy" chapter of the book. When the graves are not nearby, many genealogists rely on the "Find A Grave" website for this information, which is amazingly thorough.

HOW TO WRITE AND PUBLISH A LOCAL HISTORY BOOK

Storyline Enhancement Technique
#11 Genealogy: Engaging a Genealogy Consultant*

- Genealogy consultant researches family roots
- Expertise in ancestral village desirable
- Has access to individual ancestor records
- Editor's Email Communications Trail with consultant for clarifications
- Consultant provides a Citations and Notes Trail

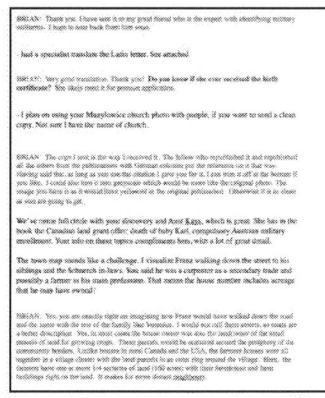

Email Communications Trail

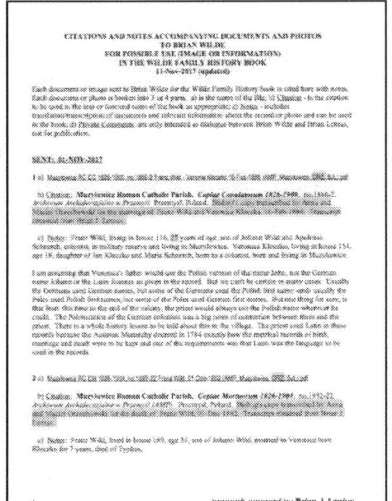

Citation and Notes Trail by Consultant

* Used in a separate case study

Storyline Enhancement Technique #11: Genealogy / Engaging a Genealogy Consultant*

A genealogy consultant can add value to a project, by having research expertise in ancestral locations with access to individual ancestor records. A consultant would need the time available to conduct specific family research requests that meet the client's schedule. Also, a consultant must exhibit the willingness and energy to join a project, in this case a book publication and the ability to contribute and add historical substance. To summarize, a consultant must have Time, Energy and Expertise.

Communications and knowledge transfer from the consultant:

- Email Communications Trail. Questions posed by the Editor and responded by the Consultant are communicated in email format. This give and take email trail records detail genealogy concepts, ancestor culture, and landmarks in the village. An email color coded format is used, with Editor text in black and Consultant guidance in blue. This format allows content to be extracted and included in the book creation process, with proper source citations to the consultant.

- Citation and Notes Communique Trail. The Consultants "Citations and Notes Trail" includes a) the source citation at the record level, on the ancestors and other pieces of genealogy information, b) notes that could be included in the book, if desired and c) private comments not meant for publication. This communique technique is instrumental in creating content provided by the consultant augmenting an Author's dialogue.

- Endnotes. Many consultants recommend detailed endnotes be placed in the book as measure of professionalism in genealogy documentation. The Editor provides endnotes for the entire book in the Appendix. This is a best practice to cite consultant content and all other relevant citations in the endnotes.

Endnotes, although a detailed and time intensive, was adhered in the *West Seven Stars and Beyond* book. It is is typically appreciated by the reader.

* Note: a consultant was not engaged for the *West Seven Stars and Beyond* book project. The Editor has used consultants in past projects.

Storyline Enhancement Technique
#12 Genealogy: The Wedding Attendees*

- Out of all key life events; weddings are one of the most joyous.
- The next best thing to being there, is finding the wedding date of a key ancestor (mid 1800's) and determining the attendees at the wedding; their ages, marital status and children at the time
- This technique could be utilized to visualize an ancestor wedding
- The chart at right is a byproduct of a wedding analysis.
- Concept is an ancestor centered life capturing everything the ancestor touched and saw
- The analysis becomes input for The Wedding Attendees Writeup (next)

The Wedding Attendees Analysis Chart is the basis for the storyline writeup.

* Used in separate case study

Storyline Enhancement Technique #12: Genealogy / The Wedding Attendees*

In this Storyline Enhancement Technique, we ask the reader to visualize the wedding between ancestors on their wedding day. From calendar math calculations using siblings birth, marriage and death records, one can determine who was likely at the wedding; their martial status, the number of children, and whether they remained in the village in later life.

Headings on Wedding Attendees Analysis Chart:
    Name: ancestor name
    Birth: date, to calculate age at wedding
    Age: year, age at time of wedding
    Information: ancestor siblings and children at the time of the wedding
    Attended wedding: yes/no based of the analysis

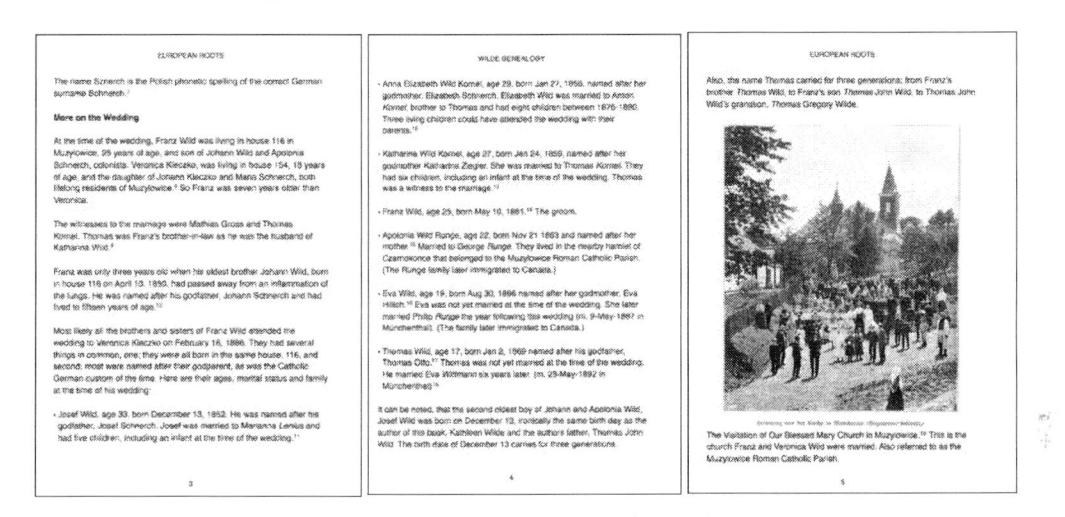

Storyline Enhancement Technique #12 (cont'd): Genealogy / The Wedding Attendees Storyline*

An example of a writeup resulting from the Wedding Attendees Enhancement Technique.

An excerpt: "Katharina Wild Kornel, age 27, born Jan, 1859, named after her godmother Katharina Ziegler. She was married to Thomas Kornel. They had six children, including an infant at the time of the wedding. Thomas was a witness to the marriage." It was also stated when the family immigrated to America.

The vintage church photo is the Visitation of the Blessed Mary Church in Munchenthal, Galicia, where the wedding was held.

Storyline Enhancement Technique
#13 Genealogy: The Shared Voyage Account*

Ancestors aboard The S.S. Arcadia ship of the Hamburg-Amerika Line was ready to set sail for Canada on April 10, 1897. The family travelled steerage class on the S.S. Arcadia, the part of the passenger ship allotted to passengers paying the lowest fare ... Dmytro Romanchych, was on the same voyage and same class (steerage) as ancestor Veronica and her three young boys.

His first hand account of the perils of traveling across the Atlantic was recorded and published in Early Ukrainian Settlements in Canada 1895-1900 by Vladimir J. Kayne (University of Toronto Press, 1964.)

Emigrants boarding a ship at the Port of Hamburg, Germany

* Used in separate case study

Storyline Enhancement Technique #13: Genealogy / The Shared Voyage Account*

This Storyline Enhancement Technique is a cultural irony; the Shared Voyage Account. Recounting from the book, *Wilde Genealogy*, the widow Veronica Wild with her three sons travelling steerage class on the S.S. Arcadia of the Hamburg Amerika Line in 1897. But she was not alone...

Dmytro Romanchych was on the same voyage on April 10, 1897 and wrote an extensive account of the challenges they faced, including ice storms and terrible sanitary conditions.

Specifically Dmytro observed • sleeping on the lower decks packed on iron bedsteads • high humidity and resulting body stench • took 21 days to get from Hamburg, Germany to Montreal, Quebec • hurricane weather and a "deluge of rain" • many became seasick, two persons died; an old man and a child and • stuck in an ice storm for three days.

Storyline Enhancement Technique #13 Genealogy: A First Hand Account of the Shared Voyage (cont'd)*

Resulting text from the first hand account of the voyage by Dmytro Romanchych, describing hurricane weather and a "deluge of rain" during the 21 day voyage across the ocean. Since the ancestor was on the same voyage, she and her boys experienced the same conditions.

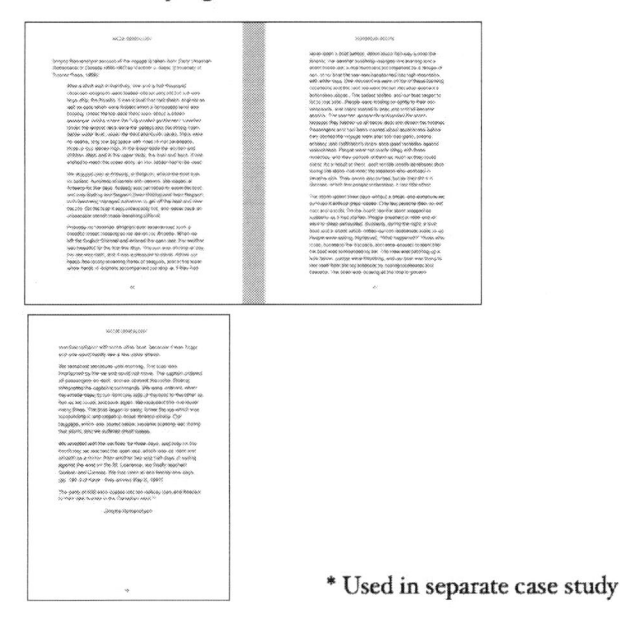

* Used in separate case study

Storyline Enhancement Technique #13 (cont'd): Genealogy / A First Hand Account of the Shared Voyage*

This resulted in an interesting addition to the book with a recorded view of the identical voyage as the ancestor. We assume the ancestor did not know Dmytro Romanchych, the storyteller, but may have seen him on the boat, since they were in the same class of service.

An excerpt: "When about half-way across the Atlantic, the weather suddenly changed one evening and a storm broke out, a real hurricane accompanied by a deluge of rain. In no time the sea was transformed into high mountains with white tops. One moment we were on top of these foaming mountains and the next we were thrown into what seemed a bottomless abyss...The ballast shifted, and our boat began to list to one side...People were holding on tightly to their iron bedsteads, and many started to pray, and until all became seasick." - Dmytro Romanchych

Storyline Enhancement Technique
#14 Genealogy: Sharing Knowledge from Consultant*

Knowledge gained when engaging a consultant are shared in the book, with the consultants agreement.

This can be for domestic or European ancestral villages, where consultants can share their knowledge on the life and times of our ancestors.

As an example, from a separate case study, the consultant hired provided the following:
- Village map with family house numbers
- "Defining our German Colony"
- Meaning of the village name
- Reasons for emigration (free land)
- Travel documents in the 19th century
- The German Catholic Cemetery Memorial
- "Family Ethnicity Explained"
- Tours of ancestral towns

Editor and wife tour of German ancestral town.

* Used in separate case study

Storyline Enhancement Technique #14: Genealogy / Sharing Knowledge from Consultant*

> - Knowledge for the sake of knowledge; that is Curiosity.
> - Knowledge to be known by others; that is Vanity.
> - Knowledge to serve others; that is Love.
>   - St. Bernard of Clairvaux

During a time of utilizing consulting services, the team gains the consultants knowledge on the life and times of ancestors. This knowledge can serve to enrich the readers interests on details of family life and the challenges that were present at that time.

Storyline Enhancement Technique #15 Historical Newspapers

Newspaper Articles

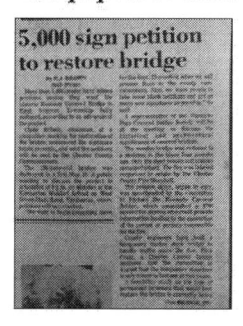

Birthday (85th) attendees list

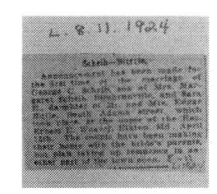

Marriage News Clip

News Accounts

Storyline Enhancement Technique #15: Historical Newspapers
The Author kept physical copies of select old newspaper articles which is rare in this age of digital transformation.

Newspaper clippings and research about South Eastern Pennsylvania are available at the Chester County Historical Society in West Chester, PA. These news clippings proved helpful for reporting the weekly Sowbelly Railroad construction progress published in the West Chester Daily Local in the mid 1890's. Also, birthday attendees lists for the Author's matriarchal mother was an intriguing find.

Storyline Enhancement Technique #16 Converting Author Interviews into Content

Hardcopy Newspaper article interview → **Digital on line newspaper article** (Potts Merc)

Eliminate attributives like:
- Scheib said ....
- Scheib suggested ...
- He stated, adding that ..
- He was quick to dispute...
- He explained...

"That was fertile ground", Scheib said.

---- becomes ----

The ground was fertile.

Storyline Enhancement Technique #16: Converting Author Interviews into Content

The Author was interviewed by The Mercury Newspaper (Potts Merc) reporter Barbara Worthington in the mid 1980's. The article was found on-line.

The interview was in the second person with Barbara asking questions and the Author responding. The questions were converted and added into the Author's response in a first person storyline.

Storyline Enhancement Technique #16 Converting Author Interviews (cont'd)

The Newspaper Reporter Interview

Was:
"People's idea of a farmer is a man with a pitchfork and a wife with a sunbonnet," Scheib said. He was quick to dispute the mistaken notion of farming in the 21st century.

Becomes:
People's idea of a farmer is a man with a pitchfork and a wife with a sunbonnet. This is the mistaken notion of farming in the 21st century.

Change from third person to first person.

Result: The interview transformed into a storyline.

Storyline Enhancement Technique #16 (cont'd): Converting Author Interviews

Result: The newspaper reporter interview became text of the Author in the first person, as if he is talking directly to the reader. All attributives relative to "Scheib" and "He said" or "He explained" were eliminated.

In the endnotes, citation credit is given to the newspaper reporter.

Storyline Enhancement Technique #17 Vintage Photos

Storyline Enhancement Technique #17: Vintage Photos
Examples of Vintage Photos. (clockwise from upper left)

Of interest are local transportation photos, in this case, a horse and carriage arrival at the Bonnie Brae Park from nearby Phoenixville PA.

The next photo shows the Author (First row 7th from left) in front of a schoolhouse and is a good example of a group photo.

The "Home of Edward Parker" photo is a residence type photo that shows the Parker's Tavern in the background and the Girard Canal in the foreground.

The Lock 56 photo, another transportation example, is courtesy of Spring-Ford Area Historical Society. The lock keepers house on the right is a private residence today.

#18 Additional Storyline Enhancement Techniques

Farm methods used by ancestors
Farm maps of property
Farm equipment of the day
History of farm ownership

Movie posters
Rededication posters
Anniversary posters
Event Posters
Sketches and hand drawn maps

Church members
Train Stations
Historical event programs
Village name history
Community oral histories
Societies, organizations, historical commissions

Train route tables
Vintage automobiles
Railroad cars
Village businesses
Founder portraits
Poems by historic figures
Animal photos
Sharing knowledge from experts
Major historical events; 1929 crash, WWII, Revolutionary War
Golden era radio programs
Landmark local history books
Historic letters
Operation of canal locks
Operation of grist mills
Arial ground views

Storyline Enhancement Technique #18: Additional Examples

This is a summary of additional storyline enhancement techniques with examples. All were used in the case study.

Technique	Example
Farm methods used by ancestors	- John Deere horse plow - McCormick reaper
Farm maps of property	Farm maps of property - Kimberton Farms property map - roads and grounds around mill race
Farm equipment of the day	- Massey Harris Farm Tractor
History of farm ownership	- Beaver Farm/ Joseph Rogers/ Dr. Beaver / Camp Hill - Kimberton Farm

Technique	Example
Movie posters	- Bright Victory movie poster
Rededication posters	- Kennedy Covered Bridge
Event Posters	- Kimberton County Fair - Luminaries at the Covered Bridge - Three Day Konclave
Anniversary posters	- 150th Birthday of Kennedy Covered Bridge
Author created map sketches	- Parker Ford and West Seven Stars sketches
Church members	- Original Centennial Evangelical Lutheran Church members
Train Stations	- French Creek Junction / Heistand; Wilson's Corner; Coventry - Delaware River and Lancaster Railroad (Sowbelly) - Pickering Valley RR Line / Kimberton Train Station - Pennsylvania Railroad / Parker Ford
Historical event programs	- Walking Tour of Old Parkerford
Village name history	- Parker Ford
Community oral histories	- Patty Moore's One Room Schoolhouse; Scheib Oral History - East Vincent Township oral histories

Technique	Example
Societies, organizations, historical commissions	- Theodore Burr Covered Bridge Society of PA - Society of Friends - Historical Society of Pennsylvania - Limerick Township Historical Society - Historical Society of the Phoenixville Area, - East Vincent Township Historical Commission - Spring-Ford Area Historical Society - Pikeland Historical Society. - Chester County Historical Society - Phoenixville Historical Society
Train route tables	- Delaware River and Lancaster Railroad (Sowbelly Railroad)
Train route tables detail (cont'd)	<table><tr><th>Station</th><th>Time</th></tr><tr><td>French Creek Junction (Pickering Valley RR connection)</td><td>-</td></tr><tr><td>Heistand</td><td>9:15</td></tr><tr><td>Wilson's Corner</td><td>9:35</td></tr><tr><td>Vincent or Red Hill</td><td>9:40</td></tr><tr><td>Sheeder</td><td>9:42</td></tr><tr><td>Boreaf (Cook's Glen)</td><td>9:45</td></tr><tr><td>Roberts</td><td>9:51</td></tr><tr><td>Pughtown</td><td>9:55</td></tr><tr><td>Coventry</td><td>10:03</td></tr><tr><td>Knauertown</td><td>10:11</td></tr><tr><td>French Creek Falls</td><td>10:15</td></tr><tr><td>Saint Peter's (Warwick Branch connection)</td><td>-</td></tr></table>
Vintage automobile photos	- 1928 Hudson with rumble seat - Five seater Maxwell
Railroad cars	- Sowbelly railroad car

Technique	Example
Village businesses	- Detwiler machine shop - Roberts Meat packing / Frankfurters napkin
Founder portraits	- Rudolf Steiner - Alarik and Mabel Myrin
Poems by historic figures	- Rudolf Steiner poem - Sarah Obertholzer poem At the Old Mill 1873 (The Mill at Anselma)
Animal photos	- cow crossing
Sharing knowledge	- biodynamic farming at 7 Stars Yogurt Farm
Major historical events	- 1929 crash - Battle of the Bulge in WWII - Revolutionary War (Battle of Brandywine painting)
Golden radio programs	- Amos and Andy; Tom Mix
Landmark local history books	- Estelle Cremers 30,000 Acres, Vincent and Pikeland Townships 1686 to 1850 - John Futhey and Gilbert Cope's (1881) History of Chester County, Pennsylvania, with genealogical and biographical sketches. - James Lockart, Sowbelly RR - The Delaware River and Lancaster Railroad (2008)

Technique	Example
Historic letters	- George Washington's letter to the President of Congress at Parker Ford; "I am now re-passing the Schuylkill at Parker's Ford with the main body of the Army ..."
Operation of canal locks	- how the gates open and boats traverse locks
Operation of grist mills	- Design of a Grist Mill; 19th century sketch
Arial ground views	- Penn Pilot historic photos of Pennsylvania (1937) for Sowbelly RR line

The Appendix: The Editor's Repository

- Professional society descriptions
- Brick wall resolutions
- Village name controversy explained
- Oral history captured by the community
- German Reformed Church cemetery
- Author's community activities
- Genealogy details and backup
- DNA Test results
- Lineage matching chart
- Event details and photos
- Ancestral village trips

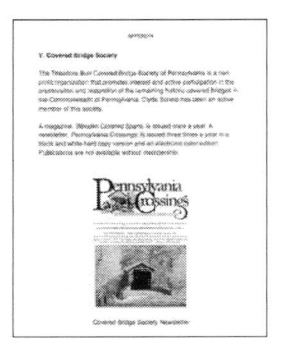

Brick Wall Resolution

Covered Bridge Society

Independence Day Event

The Appendix: The Editor's Repository

The Appendix is the Editor's repository where supplemental material are placed to help clarify the core manuscript for the reader.

Local professional societies and historical commissions at the township level are listed. Farm organizations like The Grange are described for the reader not familiar with these organizations. Another example is the Theodore Burr Covered Bridge Society of Pennsylvania that in addition to monthly meetings produces a newsletter and magazine.

Brick wall resolutions are described in the Appendix. A brick wall is a barrier to understanding the full family history. In this case study, two brick walls surfaced; one, the name of the grandparents from Europe and two; the location of the ancestral village the great grandparent were born. The resolution of these two brick walls are described in the Appendix by the Editor.

Village name controversies are explained, in this case Parker Ford Village. This allows background of the issue that is too cumbersome to include in the main manuscript. Also, village names in Pennsylvania often originate from European names, since many emigrated as a group from a European village, like the Germans that settled in this area.

Additional oral histories discovered in the content creation process qualify for the Appendix. Oral history segments relating to the storyline are captured, giving credits to the person telling the story. The oral histories in the Appendix are short in length since it had to fit within one of the topics and be a local person telling the history.

Background on historical churches, cemeteries and church events are explained by a subject matter expert, in this case study by local history professor, Dr. Robert Price.

Although Amazon has a "Authors Page" on its web site, some of the Author's accomplishments are embedded in the Appendix. In this case, these accomplishments are named: "Community Activities of Author".

The family genealogy details are described like ancestral village findings, cemetery tombstone content and additional lineage charts of family members with birth and death records.

DNA test results, although not performed in this case study, can be placed in the Appendix. This includes ethnicity details and genetic community maps, some going back 1,000 years.

Included are lineage matching charts that determine the relationship between two people; for example, two 4th cousins sharing the same ancestors, like a great grandfather.

If at a later date, European ancestral villages are explored in person, the trip findings with photos are described in the Appendix.

Endnotes and Citations
Enhancing Credibility

A biodynamic farm. Chopping corn while the sun comes up on Seven Stars Road.

- Creating citations of source material is time consuming and a major decision

- For non fiction, endnotes add credibility and offer a degree of professionalism

- Ideally, gather citations during the Create Local History phase or less desirable, compile citations at end of project.

- Using word processing superscript feature, endnote numbering (with content) can be automatically re-calibrated when new endnotes are inserted. (Apple Pages)

Endnotes by superscript number

Endnotes and Citations: Enhancing Credibility

Another aspect of the End Matter segment of the book are capturing the Endnotes. This can be time consuming to associate source with content and requires utilizing the endnotes features of the word processing package. Superscript note numbers are inserted after key sentences or images in the main storyline and the citation number and description are placed in the Appendix.

The Apple Pages word processing program is configured to automatically place the citation in the Appendix section. Another powerful Pages feature; as new endnotes are inserted, the program re-calibrates the citation numbers and moves the associated content with the new renumbered citation. This workflow process is a time saver.

Road Stories

Everything important always begins from something trivial. - Donald Hall

Book Design Example
West on Seven Stars

Introduction

Vintage photo of West Seven Stars Road looking west with Kennedy House / Kimberton Farm on right and barn on left.

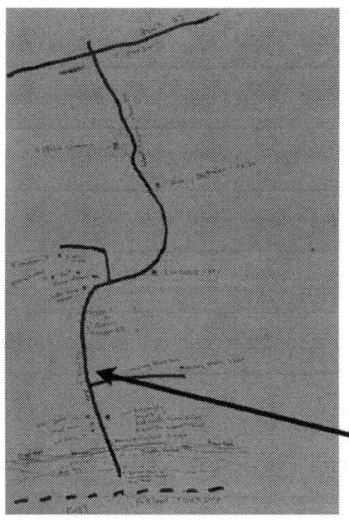

West Seven Stars Road sketch by the Author.

Author's house surrounded by history.

Book Design Example: "West on Seven Stars" / Introduction
The Author created the sketch to show the landmarks for Chapter 2 "West on Seven Stars". The dirt road is West Seven Stars Road with the Kennedy House that became the Kimberton Waldorf School.

Book Design Example
West on Seven Stars
Wheel Shop/Mill Race

Mill race depression where the water was once diverted.

Former wheel shop location (1890), later became summer house as it is today.

Bright Victory movie poster.
Movie filmed near Kennedy Covered Bridge.

Book Design Example: "West on Seven Stars" / Wheel Shop / Mill Race

An entire chapter, "West on Seven Stars", is based on a road, the West Seven Stars Road. The start of the landmarks is the wheel shop and mill race which was important to all the horse and buggy owners wanting to keep the buggy's and wagons operating.

The movie Bright Victory was released in 1951 and filmed near the summer house in Kimberton, PA and starred Arthur Kennedy and Peggy Dow. It was also filmed at Valley Forge General Army Hospital in Phoenixville, PA. It was nominated for an Academy Award. Relating history with the arts is always an interesting addition to a local story.

ROAD STORIES

Book Design Example
West on Seven Stars

Covered Bridge

Vintage cars procession on 150th Anniversary in 2006.

Rededication of the Kennedy Bridge in 1978.

West Seven Stars and Beyond
Preserving Local History

Book Design Example: "West on Seven Stars" / Covered Bridge
Historical covered bridges seem to have a life of their own. The Kennedy Covered Bridge had a colorful 150th anniversary with a parade of vintage cars. The bridge also had a rededication ceremony when it was repaired and renovated.

The greatest stories are those describing how covered bridges became a necessity to the local community. In this case study, the year was 1856, when horse and wagon transported crops through the one lane bridge.

Book Design Example
West on Seven Stars

Rudolf Steiner in 1919
(1861-1925)

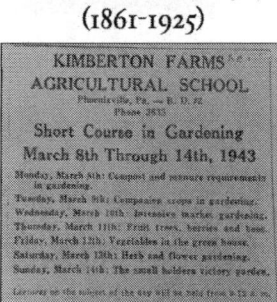

Kimberton Waldorf School

A biodynamic farm. Chopping corn while the sun comes up on Seven Stars Road.

Book Design Example: "West on Seven Stars" / Kimberton Waldorf School

The Kimberton Waldorf School has been a mainstay of the community and one the Author knows best, since he is their next door neighbor. Several photos from their history were included.

Poems make great content and the poem by Rudolph Steiner, the Waldorf founder, was included in this section.

> I look into the World
> And see the shining sun;
> I see the sparkling stars;
> I see the quiet stones;
> The plants have a life and grow;
> The beasts in feeling live;
> A dwelling their souls
> Men to the spirit give.

I look into the world
That lives within myself.

by Rudolf Steiner (Abridged)

Book Design Example
West on Seven Stars

Yogurt Farm

Seven Stars Yogurt Farm, Kimberton, PA on West Seven Stars Road. Photo by Editor.

Jersey cows at Seven Stars Yogurt Farm, with Kimberton Farms origins. Photo by Seven Stars Farm.

West Seven Stars and Beyond
Preserving Local History

Book Design Example: "West on Seven Stars" / Yogurt Farm
Seven Stars Farm is a biodynamic farm and has a history with Kimberton Farms / Kimberton Waldorf School. Several of their photos were used and their definition of "biodynamic".

A great farm photo usually involves moving animals or moving equipment on a scenic landscape of field, road, barns and house. It can be an art to get the right shot. For the Editor to capture these photos would be time consuming and he/she may never get the right moment. That is why the Seven Stars Yogurt Farm photos were all from their archives on Facebook. They really captured the moment of their farm.

Book Design Example
West on Seven Stars

Community Supported Agriculture (CSA)

Kimberton CSA, a ten acre biodynamic, organic mixed vegetable farm on West Seven Stars Road.
Photo by Kimberton CSA.

Rainbow over the Kimberton CSA.
Photo by Kimberton CSA.

West Seven Stars and Beyond
Preserving Local History

Book Design Example: "West on Seven Stars" / Community Supported Agriculture (CSA)
Another example of leveraging an establishments photo archive. In this case the Kimberton CSA Facebook archive with farm photos of a scenic field landscape and even a rainbow over the CSA. As mentioned, it is an art form to get brilliant photos like these and nearly impossible for the Editor/ Author to do so in a reasonable time frame. The photos stand out in color and is one reason to offer a color version of a book in addition to B&W.

Book Design Example West on Seven Stars — Tenant Farming

Beaver Farm at Camphill Special School

Tenant house today from West Seven Stars Road.

Beaver Farm House before electric. Sold by Joseph Rogers to Daniel Beaver in 1863.

Book Design Example: "West on Seven Stars" / Tenant Farming
This example shows how a tenant house on a farm carries stories about that era of life.

By definition: "A tenant farmer is a person who farms the land of another and pays rent with cash or with a portion of the produce". Tenants typically bring their own tools and animals. A sharecropper, on the other hand, is a tenant farmer who usually provides no capital and pays fees with crops. The Author was a tenant farmer and the Author's father started as a sharecropper.

The house photo (center) is the tenant house, built in 1926 by the Beaver family. This house, on West Seven Stars Road, was the Author's residence from 1929 to 2002 where he was a tenant farmer.

Dr. Beaver was the owner of the farm and tenant house. He was educated at MIT and was a professor at Lehigh University. He spent his summers at Beaver Farm and collected rent from the Author year round. He supplied the seed for the crops.

The Author's father moved from Birchrunville, to be a tenant farmer on this land. There were 110 acres of land with crops of corn, wheat, oats, hay and cows producing milk. Milk would be temporarily cooled and stored in the spring house and brought to Kimberton where it was cooled and placed on a train to one of several stalls at Philadelphia's Reading Market.

The Author's uncles would work the farm at harvest time cultivating corn and wheat using a manual reaper. They used horses in that era. A horse would need approximately five acres to grow the food that it consumed. The horses got tired and could only be used for 6- 8 hours per day.

Book Design Example
West on Seven Stars

Historian's Farm

Cremers house on West Seven Stars Road.

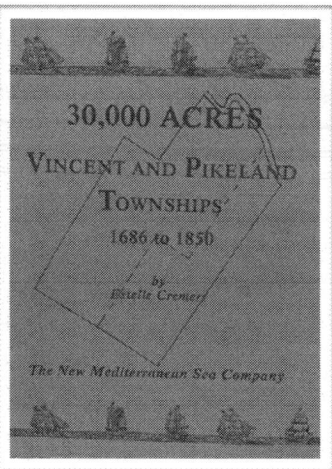

Estelle Cremers' landmark 1989 book on East Vincent and Pikeland Townships history.

Estelle Cremers, historian circa 1986.

ROAD STORIES

Book Design Example: "West on Seven Stars" / Historian's Farm
A well-known Chester County historian was Estelle Cremers. Through her work for the French and Pickering Creeks Conservation Trust and private research, she has in the past 30 years become a leading authority on the history of Northern Chester County.

She acknowledged the Author in her seminal 1989 book *30,000 Acres, Vincent and Pikeland Townships 1686 to 1850*. They were good friends. Mrs. Cremers was also an accomplished vocalist, graduating from the Curtis Institute of Music for voice. Mrs. Cremers was the soloist at Washington Memorial Chapel.

Book Design Example
West on Seven Stars

Hoffman Farm

Hoffman barn on West Seven Stars Road.

Kimberton Hunt subdivision entrance (old Hoffman Farm)

Book Design Example: "West on Seven Stars" / Hoffman Farm
Next is the Hoffman barn on West Seven Stars Road. In 1830 the farm was owned by Henry Hoffman. It is now a subdivision called Kimberton Hunt with 36 single family houses. The original farm and barn remain.

Book Design Example
West on Seven Stars

Historic Inn

Seven Stars Inn historical sketch.

Seven Stars Inn

West Seven Stars and Beyond
Preserving Local History

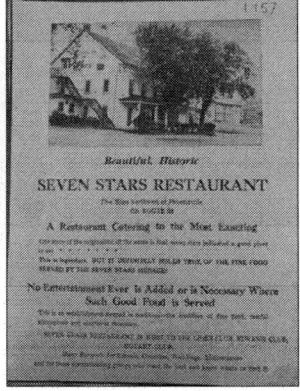

Seven Stars Inn advertisement (1957)

Book Design Example: "West on Seven Stars" / Historic Inn
The Seven Stars Inn was built in 1754 and was a resting stop on busy Route 23. Drovers with herds of cattle on the way to market would stop at the Inn while the cattle grazed in the adjacent field. People also benefited from cattle and horse auctions.

Taverns and hotels defined a rural community in those days providing rich local history storylines.

Covered Bridge Lives

The years teach much which the days never know. - Ralph Waldo Emerson

Book Design Example
Kennedy Covered Bridge 1856

Painter Sandra Giangiulio framed print hanging at East Pikeland Township Building, Chester County, Pennsylvania.

Book Design Example: Kennedy Covered Bridge (1856)

This section shares more content examples that make up the historic Kennedy Covered Bridge inclusion of "West on Seven Stars" chapter.

Book Design Example
Kennedy Covered Bridge

Luminaries

Inside Looking Out: The Kennedy Covered Bridge over the French Creek

Luminaries by The Friends of the Kennedy Covered Bridge

Book Design Example Kennedy Covered Bridge / Luminaries

The luminaries leading up to the Kennedy Covered Bridge are organized by the Author as the leader of The Friends of the Kennedy Covered Bridge. The French Creek, which the bridge crosses, is one of the cleanest creeks in Pennsylvania.

Book Design Example
Kennedy Covered Bridge

Bridge Fire 1986

Firefighters on bridge with hose.
No injuries were reported.

Fire at Kennedy Covered Bridge

Book Design Example: Kennedy Covered Bridge / Bridge Fire 1986
The fire at the Kennedy Covered Bridge was a catastrophe to the community. Residents live each day with the bridge and having it gutted was a real community loss. The cause was petty vandalism by some youth.

Book Design Example
Kennedy Covered Bridge

Rebuild Petition

Temporary Kennedy Covered Bridge operated for two years.

Petition to restore bridge started by Author.

Book Design Example: Kennedy Covered Bridge / Rebuild Petition
The Author took this loss to heart and organized a petition to restore the historic Kennedy Covered Bridge. For several years a temporary bridge was used to cross the French Creek.

COVERED BRIDGE LIVES

Book Design Example
Kennedy Covered Bridge

Rebuild Covered Bridge

Rebuilding the Kennedy Covered

Book Design Example: Kennedy Covered Bridge / Rebuild Covered Bridge
The rebuild of the bridge used bongossi wood, a specialty non burning wood from West Africa. So there should be no further bridge fires.

Book Design Example
Kennedy Covered Bridge

Bridge 150th Anniversary

Kennedy Covered Bridge today

Kennedy Covered Bridge 150th Anniversary

Book Design Example: Kennedy Covered Bridge / Bridge 150th Anniversary
The bridge with birthday parties and anniversaries. A ceremony with speakers for the 150th anniversary of the Kennedy Covered Bridge. This historic bridge is a reminder of the local history to all that cross it daily.

Unearthing a Historic Village

I was brought up telling stories, when I was a kid, in the tiny village where I grew up. Storytelling was a tradition. - Peter Stormare

Book Design Example
Parker Ford Village

Landmarks Map

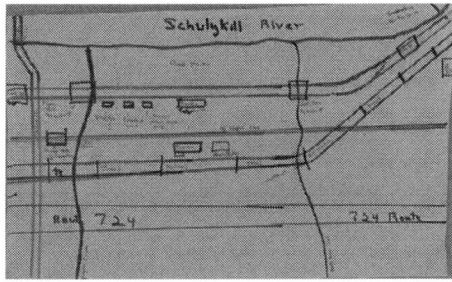

Parker Ford Village landmarks sketch by Author. (2019)

Aerial view of Parker Ford Village at right with Girard Canal depression visible.

HOW TO WRITE AND PUBLISH A LOCAL HISTORY BOOK

Book Design Example: "Parker Ford Village" / Landmarks Map
The aerial view of Parker Ford Village with Girard Canal depression visible is taken from the Parker Ford Historic Park Conceptual Plan, 2019.

This is how the *West Seven Stars and Beyond* book project got its start. The Editor was a member of the task force providing input into the Parker Ford Historic Park Conceptual Plan for a new trail and park. The team reached out to historian Clyde Scheib (The Author) for his knowledge on the Parker Ford Village.

A current day walking tour of Parker Ford Village was conducted by the Editor and the Author. The resulting Parker Ford landmark sketch (previous page) by the Author was presented to the task force. Additionally, the photos taken from the historical walking tour were also presented.

This section shares content examples that make up the chapter on the historic "Parker Ford Village".

Book Design Example
Parker Ford Village

Historic District

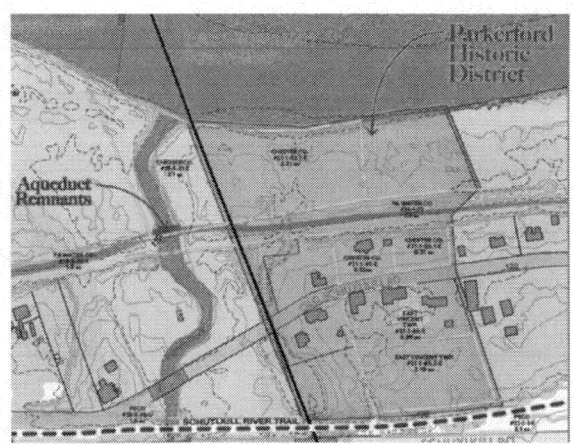

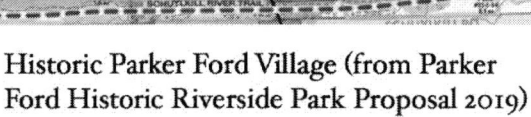

Historic Parker Ford Village (from Parker Ford Historic Riverside Park Proposal 2019)

Book Design Example: "Parker Ford Village" / Historic District

Parker Ford Village is a historic district on the Schuylkill River and Girard Canal. A conceptual plan for a new trail and park was created. The diagram (previous page) is the current layout of the area within East Coventry and East Vincent Townships. The area dates back to the 1700's and the Revolutionary War.

Book Design Example
Parker Ford Village

Girard Canal

Lock 56 Parker Ford Village

Girard Canal embankment

Book Design Example "Parker Ford Village" / Girard Canal

Lock 56 and the Lockhouse was an important part of the the Girard Canal. Although not shown here, the current house is a private residence and can be compared to this vintage Lockhouse photo as a way of presenting a "Then and Now" comparison.

The green grass embankment shows where the Girard Canal once flowed. The Girard Canal is the longest section (22 miles) of the Schuylkill Navigation System (108 miles) that ran from Pottsville to Philadelphia. To history buffs, this is high on the list of an interesting slackwater navigation systems of the 1820's.

Book Design Example
Parker Ford Village

Aqueduct

Pigeon Creek Aqueduct. This aqueduct was constructed to carry the new canal over Pigeon Creek.

Vintage photo of canal and boat.

Book Design Example: "Parker Ford Village" / Aqueduct
Schuylkill River Navigation Company and the Girard Canal remnants include the canal, towpath and aqueduct shown above that enabled the canal to cross over Pigeon Creek.

Excerpt from the nomination document for Park Ford, National Register of Historic Places, 1982:

"In 1824 the Schuylkill River Canal made Parker's Ford part of a regional system of waterways that supplied Philadelphia with coal from the northern counties. As the railroad flourished and canal trade slackened, the Parker's Ford complex was doomed to disuse and decay."

Today, it is undergoing a renewed interest in it's historical transportation storyline.

Book Design Example
Parker Ford Village

Historic Tavern

Parker's Tavern built in 1766

Parker's Tavern side view.

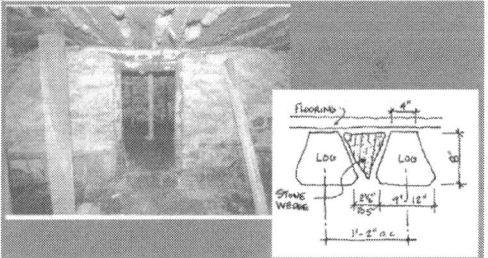

Basement Parker's Tavern

Book Design Example: "Parker Ford Village" / Historic Tavern
After the "Battle of the Clouds" General George Washington retreated to Parker Ford while preparing to cross the Schuylkill River. Washington used the Parkers Tavern as a temporary headquarters as his troops struggled with crossing the river swollen by heavy rainfall. Washington was racing to beat General Howe to Philadelphia.

From the nomination document for Parker Ford, National Register of Historic Places,1982: "Located on what was once the "Great Road" from Philadelphia to Reading, the tavern offers an insight into the social and commercial dependencies that developed between the complex and travelers."

The Tavern is currently owned by East Vincent Township in Chester County, Pennsylvania.

Book Design Example — Parker Ford Village — Houses Facing Canal

Parkers House (Ann Tudor House) with Girard Canal in foreground, Parkers Tavern in background.

Parkers House (Ann Tudor House) with steps to canal embankment.

Book Design Example: "Parker Ford Village" / Houses Facing Canal

Although no survey of the Parker House (aka Ann Tudor House) house has been completed, the building appears to be in good condition. The house is currently vacant. It is owned by Chester County.

The house is proposed to be repurposed as a park headquarters and exhibit hall for information regarding the history of Parker Ford village, including the Tavern and Girard Canal section of the Schuylkill Navigation Company network. It may also function as a staging area for guided tours of the Parkerford Tavern and village history in the future.

Book Design Example
Parker Ford Village

Horse Stables

Stables building next to Parker's Tavern.

Stables next to Parkers Tavern. Entrance still showing.

Book Design Example: "Parker Ford Village" / Horse Stables
The History Walking Tour proved to be an excellent way for the Author to get reacquainted with the village in the modern time and share his history with the Editor. From the tour were photos of the two story colonial building that served as a horse barn next to Parker's Tavern. It was able to accommodate 30 horses according to newspaper clippings from the 1850's. Remnants of the stables arch can be seen.

Book Design Example
Parker Ford Village
Life in the Village

Looking East Main Road, Parker Ford PA

Eureka Hall and High School

Parker Ford Post Office 1905

Roberts Bridge Pigeon Creek Parker Ford PA
- Angela Lupo

Book Design Example: "Parker Ford Village" / Life in the Village
These Parker Ford Village vintage photos give a glimpse at rural life in the 19th century. The photos were captured by iPhone from the Parker Ford Post Office lobby, behind a locked display cabinet. Credits went to Angela Lupo of Parker Ford, PA.

UNEARTHING A HISTORIC VILLAGE

Book Design Example
A Proposal for a New Historic Parker Ford Village

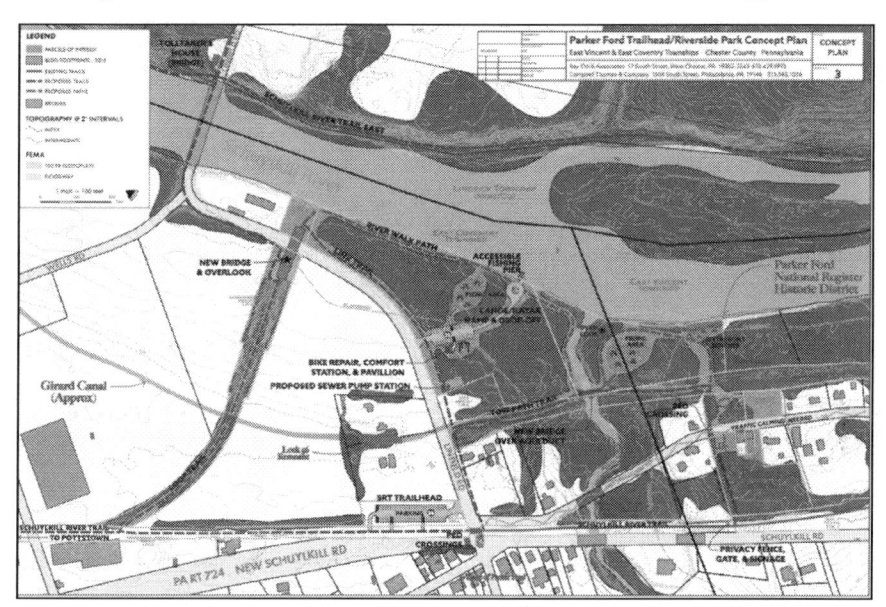

Conceptual Plan

Parker Ford Historic Park Conceptual Plan 2019. Frick's Lock and Tow Path Park in East Coventry Township are north of this site.

Book Design Example: "Parker Ford Village" / Conceptual Plan
A proposed park at Parkers Ford includes nearly 14 acres owned among Chester County, East Coventry and East Vincent Townships. The plan is to have the Schuylkill River Trail loop through a new park.

From The Parker Ford Historic Park Conceptual Plan 2019:

"Create a riverside park within the context of the historic Parker Ford Village and remnants of the Girard Canal section of the Schuylkill Navigation Company system. Also provide public access to the Schuylkill River for non-motorized boating and an accessible fishing pier."

"The goal is to promote appreciation of the site's historic resources: including the Parker Ford Tavern and the Girard Canal – the longest section of the Schuylkill Navigation Company system that ran from Pottsville to Philadelphia. Also, provide a direct link to the Schuylkill River Trail and the proposed Schuylkill River East Trail in Montgomery County."

Historical restoration outlined in a Township Master Plan:

"The 2005 Master Plan for the Parkerford Tavern prepared by Frens and Frens Restoration Architects recommends several options to essentially operate the tavern as a museum. As noted in the report, the Parkerford Tavern is of exceptional historical value because it has been relatively unchanged since it was built in 1766."

"The proposed building work objective is for the tavern 'To be stabilized and interpreted as an unrestored historic building.' The tavern never had a kitchen, bathroom or central heating and only minimal surface mounted electrical wiring."

Genealogy at the Cemetery

> We all carry inside us, people who came before us. - Liam Callanan

Book Design Example: Genealogy — Ancestral Village

Clyde Vernon Scheib

Alda Wenger Scheib

Glarus Switzerland is Clyde's ancestral village, grandmother's side.

Backnang, Germany is Clyde's ancestral village, grandfather's side.

Book Design Example: Genealogy
Genealogy and family history are closely related and in some respect the terms are considered synonyms. The Scheib family history was researched to add another aspect to local history.

Book Design Example
Where is the Scheib Ancestral Village?

Brick Wall

St. Matthews Cemetery

Christinna C. (1822-1875) is the wife of John J. Scheib

Christinna C. Scheib village name on gravestone: Siebenknie O.A. Baknanc Wurttemberg.

Generations of the Scheib family from Wurttemberg Germany

Book Design Example: Genealogy / Brick Wall
The European ancestral village of the Scheib family was unknown and was one of two brick walls or roadblocks to further understanding.

In the St. Matthews Luthern Church Cemetery, the tombstone of Christinna Scheib (John J. Scheib's wife) showed the exact location where she was born: Siebenknie, Baknang, Wurttemberg, Germany.

Note the misspelling on the Christinna Scheib tombstone of "Baknang" which today is Backnang. Siebenknie is a village in the Backnang district of Baden- Wurttemberg. The kingdom of Wurttemberg was a German state that existed from 1805 to 1918. The Scheib family in Europe lived in the Backnang district near the village of Siebenknie, in current day Germany.

Book Design Example
Who are David Scheib's Parents?

Brick Wall

Certificate of Death. David Jasper Scheib (Feb 15, 1836 - Jan 30, 1919) Born in Germany. David is Clyde Scheib's grandfather.

David J. Scheib parents are shown as **Frederick & Elizabeth** Scheib from Germany. They would be Clyde Scheib's great grandfather.

Certificate of Death. Margaretta Kubley Scheib (July 4, 1860 - Feb 3, 1952). Margaretta is Clyde Scheib's grandmother.

Margaretta (Margarita) birthplace is shown here as Glarus, Switzerland.

Book Design Example: Genealogy / Brick Wall
Death certificates are valuable in determining not only birth and death dates, but parents names, residence and home towns. In this case, David Scheib parents are named, resulting in smashing the brick wall. Now the parents are known to this generation of the Scheib family.

Book Design Example
Genealogy Lineage Chart - Scheib

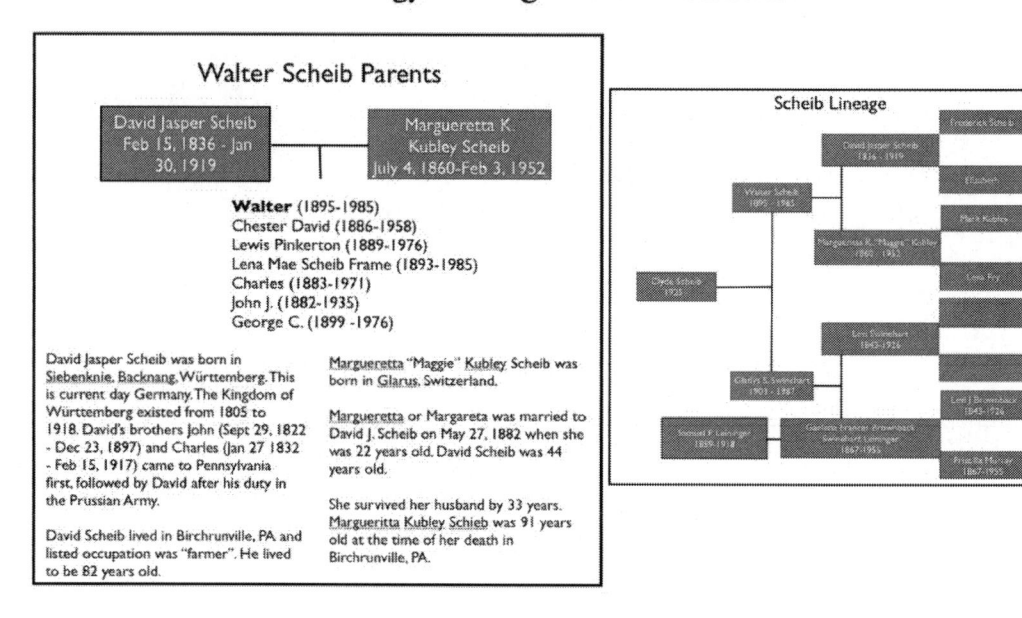

Lineage Chart

Walter Scheib Parents

David Jasper Scheib
Feb 15, 1836 - Jan 30, 1919

Margueretta K. Kubley Scheib
July 4, 1860 - Feb 3, 1952

Walter (1895-1985)
Chester David (1886-1958)
Lewis Pinkerton (1889-1976)
Lena Mae Scheib Frame (1893-1985)
Charles (1883-1971)
John J. (1882-1935)
George C. (1899 -1976)

David Jasper Scheib was born in Siebenknie, Backnang, Württemberg. This is current day Germany. The Kingdom of Württemberg existed from 1805 to 1918. David's brothers John (Sept 29, 1822 - Dec 23, 1897) and Charles (Jan 27 1832 - Feb 15, 1917) came to Pennsylvania first, followed by David after his duty in the Prussian Army.

David Scheib lived in Birchrunville, PA and listed occupation was "farmer". He lived to be 82 years old.

Margueretta "Maggie" Kubley Scheib was born in Glarus, Switzerland.

Margueretta or Margareta was married to David J. Scheib on May 27, 1882 when she was 22 years old. David Scheib was 44 years old.

She survived her husband by 33 years. Margueritta Kubley Schieb was 91 years old at the time of her death in Birchrunville, PA.

Scheib Lineage

Book Design Example: Genealogy / Lineage Chart

The lineage chart developed by the Editor is a method to show lineage from one generation to another and the family member relationships, known and unknown. This serves as a baseline for family research in a future generation. Typically, one member of a generation becomes the family history guardian.

The Author was born in Birchrunville and lived ninety plus years on the same road. The Scheib name has been a fixture in local history for several generations.

Book Design Example
Genealogy Lineage Chart - Swinehart

Lineage Chart

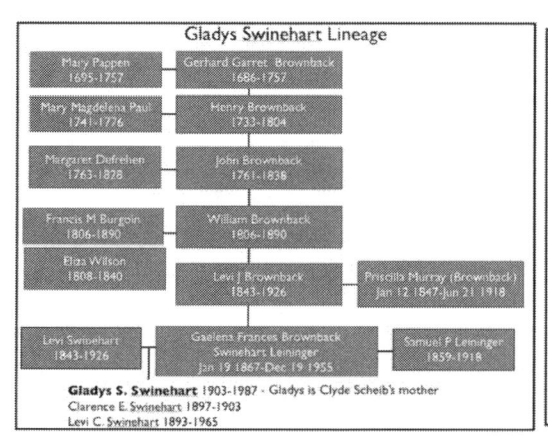

Gladys Swinehart is Clyde Scheib's mother. Gladys mother was Gaelena Brownback. The Author has Brownback lineage.

The Patriarch: William Brownback, Clyde Scheib's Great Great Grandfather.

Book Design Example: Genealogy / Lineage Chart
The Brownbacks are shown as part of the Swinehart family tree. The Patriarch: William Brownback is the Author's Great Great Grandfather.

The "Brownback" name is a well known name in the community. The Author's Great Grandmother was Priscilla Murray Brownback (1846-1918). There are many remnants of the Brownbacks in the area, including buildings, churches and cemeteries. An entire chapter in the book *West Seven Stars and Beyond* is dedicated to explaining the Scheib family genealogy.

Book Design Example: Genealogy / Lineage Chart
Discovered on ancestor.com is a photo of the Swinehart family. This is combined with the lineage chart adds a face with the name.

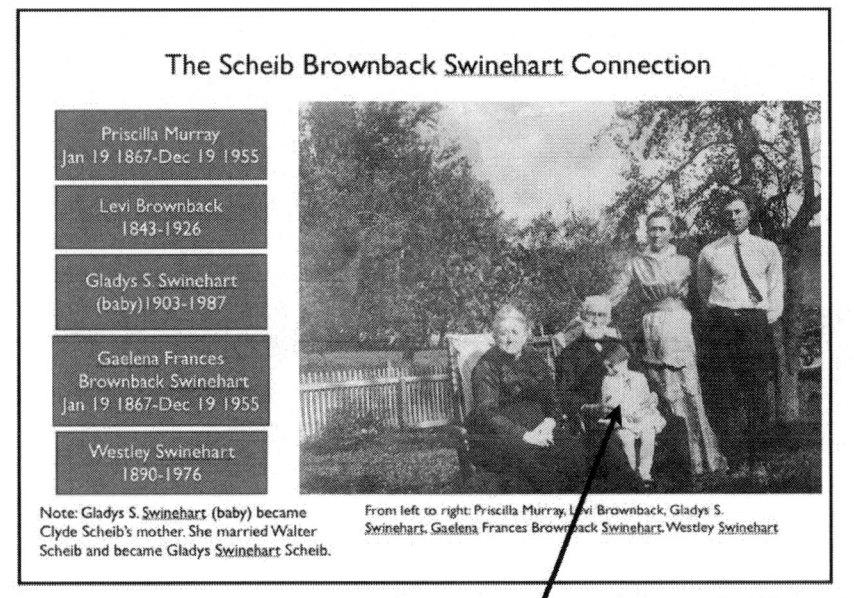

Book Design Example
Scheib German Roots

Ancestral Village

Backnang town center in Germany. Backnang is also a district. Nearby, the ancestral village of Siebenknie, where Christina C. Scheib was born on Jan 26, 1822. She is wife of John J. Scheib.

The Scheib ancestral village is near Siebenknie, Backnang, Württemberg, Germany. David Scheib came to Pennsylvania after his duty in the Prussian Army.

Book Design Example: Genealogy / Ancestral Village
Here is a view and location of the Scheib ancestral village of Siebenknie, Backnang, Württemberg, Germany. By resolving the ancestral village brick wall, further research on the village is possible.

Book Design Example
Scheib Swiss Roots

Ancestral Village

Glarus, Switzerland

Glarus, Switzerland where Margueritta K. "Maggie" Kubley was born on July 4, 1860 to Mark and Lena Fry Kubley. Maggie is Clyde Scheib's grandmother.

Book Design Example: Genealogy / Ancestral Village
Glarus, Switzerland is where Margueritta K. "Maggie" Kubley was born on July 4, 1860 to Mark and Lena Fry Kubley. Maggie is the Author's grandmother.

Deliverable

> Just get it down on paper, and then we'll see what to do with it.
> - Maxwell Perkins

Content Creation Deliverable: The Digital Document (PDF)

- Follow a standardized "Table Of Contents" book structure
- "Forward" by Editor
- "Introduction" by Author
- Chapters with Storyline Enhancements
- Appendix for support documents
- Bibliography from research
- Acknowledgments by Author
- Endnotes with main body citation number
- Images supporting and enhancing the storyline
- Document proofread and edited
- Gain Author approval
- Print ready format (PDF)

Next step: "Self Publish the Book"

Table of Contents

Foreword

Introduction

Chapter 1.	Brief History of Kimberton	1
Chapter 2.	West on Seven Stars	31
Chapter 3.	Parker Ford Village	81
Chapter 4.	Living with Sowbelly	115
Chapter 5.	My One Room Schoolhouse	147
Chapter 6.	Underground Railroad	181
Chapter 7.	Bonnie Brae Park	199
Chapter 8.	Scheib Genealogy	209
Chapter 9.	Farming Life	219
Chapter 10.	Two Forgotten Names	229
Chapter 11.	Unknown Soldiers	247

Appendix . 257

Bibliography . 293

Acknowledgments . 295

Endnotes . 297

Book Structure Table of Contents

Content Creation Deliverable: The Digital Document (PDF)

The manuscript follows a standardized book structure acceptable in publishing best practices. This includes Front Matter (Foreword, Introduction), Content (Chapters) and Back Matter (Appendix, Bibliography, Acknowledgements and Endnotes).

Several sources are used: a) "The Parts of a Book for Self Publishers" by Joel Friedlander, b) "Self Publishing: How to Organize the Components of Your Book" (GlobalGenealogy.com) by Rick Roberts and c) "Parts of a Book for Self Published Authors" at Writersandeditors.com.

In this case study, the Forward is created by the Editor and the Introduction by the Author.

Content Creation Deliverable: The Digital Document (PDF)

"Parts of a Book for Self Publishing Authors" by Writersandeditors.com

The 1734 Spring House at The Mill at Anselma in Chester Springs, PA. One solid structure that has withstood the ravishes of time.

Once all research and content is complete, and the Author approves the word processing document and the print ready PDF document is prepared to close out Unpacking Memories.

Summary

Unpacking Memories of Chapter 1 showed the techniques used in creating content for a local history book. Several design examples were shared including Road Stories, Covered Bridge Lives, Unearthing a Historic Village and Genealogy at the Cemetery. Road Stories showed how one road defined the Author's concept of local history.

Next we show how the book is organized within a standardized book structure; the front matter, content and back matter. The book is formatted and the blank and full page spacing completed. Now the case study enters the Book Construction Zone.

Chapter 2. Book Construction Zone

The cool thing about writing music, writing anything, is that once you publish it, it's there forever. - Ryan Tedder

Self Publish the Book

Self Publish the Book
With the print ready PDF document, the Editor begins the process of self publishing the local history book using Amazon's Kindle Direct Publishing (KDP) software.

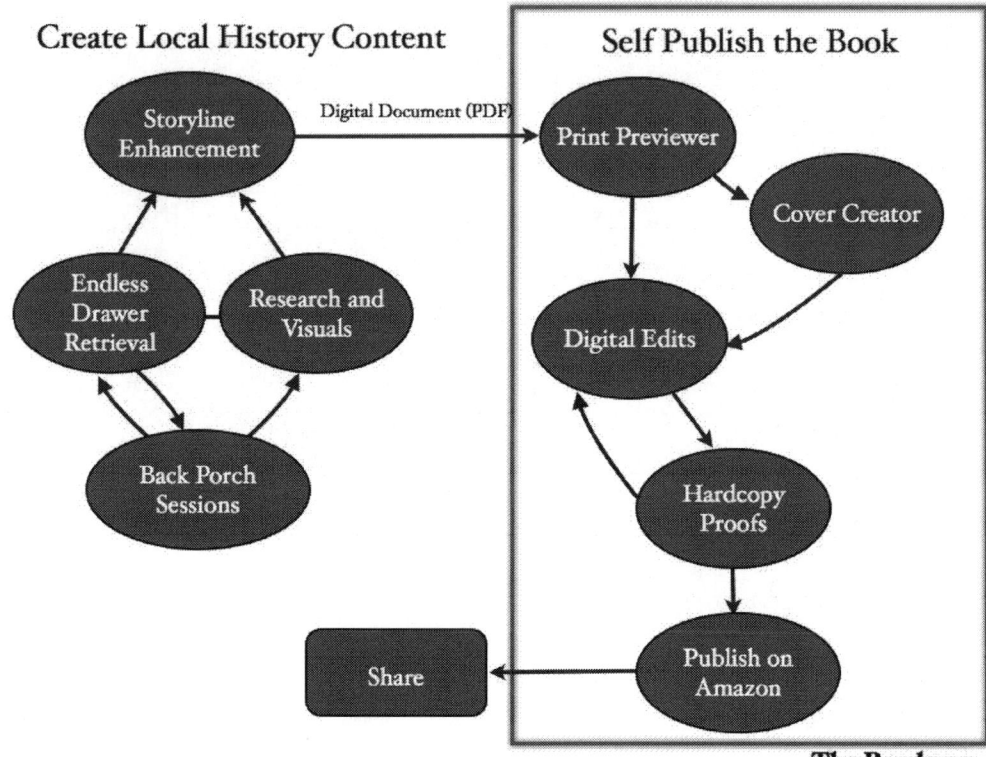

Create Local History Content / Self Publish the Book

The Roadmap

Self Publish the Book / The Roadmap

Shown are the steps of the Roadmap to Self Publish the Book. Once all research is completed, the print ready Digital Document (PDF) from the Create Local History Content process is prepared for migration to the self publishing digital reader (Print Previewer); complete with page, section and chapter formatting.

The publishing process continues with creating a front and back book cover, in this case using Lulu's software cover creator templates. The Amazon KDP cover creator could be used as well.

The publishing process on Amazon KDP begins with set up and content validation. Once digital edits and content validation is complete, a hardcopy proof is ordered from Amazon. A proof is a draft of the book for review by the Editor and Author.

If the hardcopy proof has errors and requires further edits, it is recommended the process be repeated; modify manuscript, create an updated Digital Document (PDF), transfer to the Print Previewer and reorder another proof.

When the proof copy is acceptable to the Author, the publishing on Amazon continues with setting the price, determining distribution channels and creating the Amazon page description. The book is then submitted to Amazon for approval to publish. Within 3 days, if approved, the book is published and available for purchase.

A good practice is to set up the "Authors Page", which can be done while the book is being reviewed by Amazon or at a later date, since it is not contingent on the book being published.

Publishing Software

On-line Software:
- Amazon Kindle Direct Publishing (KDP)
- Lulu
- BookBaby

Software Differentiators:

- Lulu - hardcover and paperback
- Amazon - paperback only, no hardcover

- All offer ebooks.

- Timeframe to get Lulu titles to Amazon platform (2-4 weeks)
- Timeframe to get KDP title to Amazon platform (3-4 days)

- BookBaby has hard cover coffee table book

- Best Digital Proofer - Kindle Direct Publishing (Amazon)

- Best Cover Creator - Lulu

Publishing Software
The best of breed self publishing companies used on this project were Amazon's Kindle Direct Publishing (KDP), Lulu and Bookbaby. The largest differentiator is that Amazon offers a paperback book with no

hardcover option; whereas Lulu and BookBaby offer both hardcover and paperback books. If you are planning to create a hardcover coffee table type book, your vendor selection is narrowed to Lulu and BookBaby. All offer ebooks.

Since Lulu and BookBaby are outside the Amazon ecosystem, it takes longer (2-4 weeks) to get a book published on Amazon. If Amazon KDP is used to create content, a book can be published on it's Amazon platform in as little as three to five days.

The Editor can create physical proofs from several software platforms to compare the type, end product, quality and value.

The Editors view: the best digital proofer is Amazon's Print Previewer and the best Cover Creator is from Lulu. This is for a B&W (Black & White) or color perfect bound paperback book.

Publishing the Book

Book Specifications:

- Book types
paperback, hardcover, ebook

- Book Trim Size
8.5" x 11"
7.44" x 9.68"

- Color vs. Black and White
- covers are always in color
- interior: **color** or **black and white**

- Distribution
- **Amazon** vs Lulu
- all offer Print on Demand (POD)
- all offer bulk orders

Note: **Bold** used on this project.

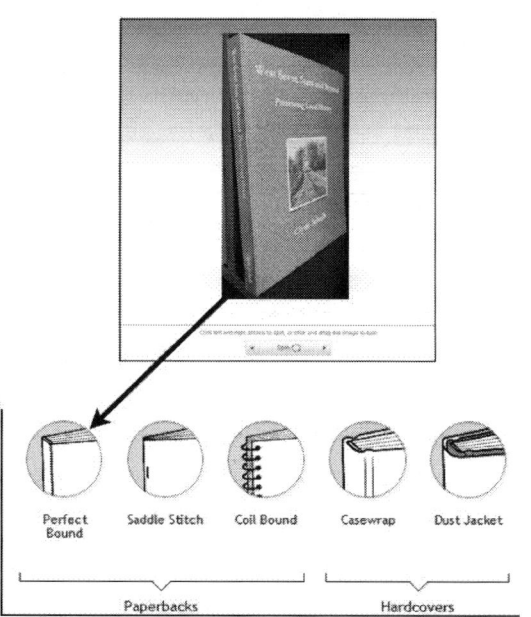

Book bindings options. Perfect bound was used for the book *West Seven Stars and Beyond*.

Details on Publishing the Book
The book types are paperback, hardcover and ebook.

The book trim size for this project was 7.44" x 9.68" since the size is easy to handle and read. It's best to start with the final book trim size versus the standard 8.5" x 11" trim size. Otherwise, reformatting of text and image for the entire manuscript is required to get into the final trim size.

The book covers are always in color, unless a vintage B&W photo is used for historical effect. The interior can be B&W or color.

Note, the color interior can be three to four times the cost of a B&W book. The reason is each page, whether an image or text, is treated as a color page, which increases the printing cost of the book. Since vintage photos by their nature do not benefit from color enhancements, B&W interior has advantages for a local history book. A color interior can be offered at a greater price in addition to the B&W book. Both are paperback books using the popular perfect bound book binding.

The ideal coffee table book, would be color exterior, color interior and a hardcover trim. This can be accomplished with either Lulu or BookBaby. Both case wrap and dust jacket bindings are good choices for hardcover books. A case wrap hardcopy proof was ordered and evaluated from BookBaby, a full service publishing company. The hardcopy proof was impressive.

Print-on-Demand (POD) from a self publishing company means every order is a custom order. Books are not printed until the order is placed, so small quantities can be ordered, printed and shipped for each customer order. It is possible to order bulk copies from the companies as well.

The Cover Creator

Lulu Cover Creator

- Both Kindle Direct Publishing and Lulu have cover creators.
- Lulu cover template selected
- Using a template is the fastest method to get book published
- Professionally designed covers are available through 3rd parties (not used in this case study)
- Warning sign exclamations (!) is for low resolution. Continue with warning sign.
- UPC bar code generated by Lulu will be overwritten by Amazon KDP
- **End result**: upload Lulu created cover into Amazon KDP software

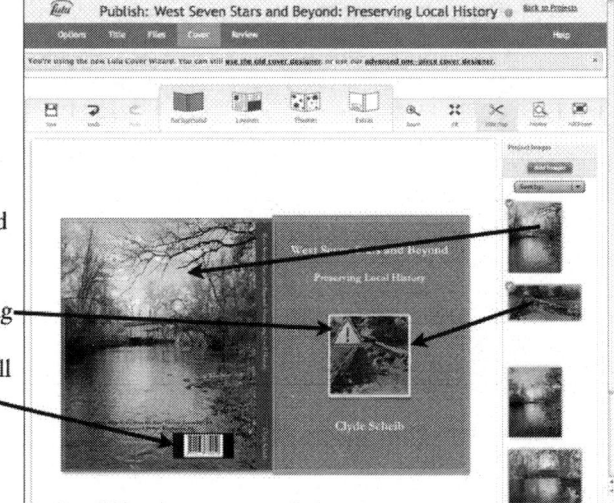

Lulu generated cover with personalized images on the right placed into the cover template

Closer Look: The Cover Creator

The two cover creators considered on this project are Lulu and Amazon KDP. Many opt to have a third party cover design specialist create their cover for a cost. For this project, the best cover creator template was Lulu, primarily for speed, ease of use and functionality.

As shown, images are imported into the Lulu Cover Creator and moved onto the cover from the right side of the tool. The Lulu specific bar code ISBN (International Standard Book Number) resides on the back cover in an industry-wide standard position. The Lulu cover is next exported as a PDF. When importing the cover into the Amazon software, the Amazon specific ISBN bar code number overrides and replaces the Lulu ISBN bar code exactly.

The yield warning sign shown on the front image (with an exclamation point) is a low resolution warning that 300 dpi was not attained. This can be ignored. Low resolution in this case is due to the vintage nature of the photo.

Amazon KDP Publishing Process

- SetUp
  1) title, ISBN, interior
  2) color, trim

- Upload Interior
- Upload Cover

- Content Validation
  1) using Print Previewer
  2) using PDF Proofer

- Order hardcopy proof
- Set price
- Set distribution channels
- Description for Amazon page
- Review proof with Author
- Approve by Author/Editor
- Publish to Amazon.com
- Set up Authors Page

Print Previewer

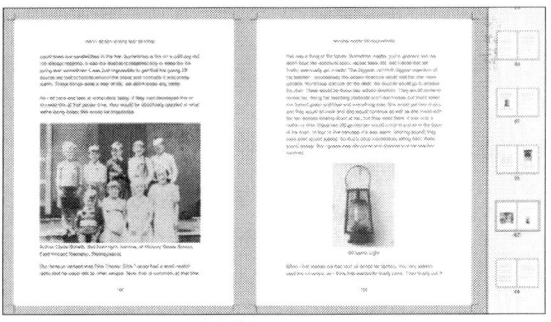

PDF Proofer

Amazon KDP Publishing Process

The Amazon book creation process includes account set up, interior upload and cover upload. The ISBN is generated as a free service by Amazon. The paid ISBN option available at Amazon through Bowker, allows the Editor to use other publishers and distributors outside of Amazon's ecosystem.

There are two preview methods for editing, both can be used prior to publishing. These content validation tools are the Print Previewer and the PDF Proofer. These tools show out-of-alignment error messages with images and text placement on the digital page.

a. Print Previewer

This method is required to move into the publishing phase of the KDP software. This shows how the book will look in a digital format. If major issues occur, the Print Previewer will not let you proceed to the next section until corrected. Minor issues and quality checks are noted and automatically fixed by the software to allow moving to the next segment of the publishing process.

Amazon KDP Print Previewer

- Upload print ready cover (PDF) into Amazon software
- Edit page format, page headings, numbering

b. The PDF Proofer
The PDF proofer is an option to view the content in a digital book format. No error messages are shown, so it is the raw book as it would look published. It is best to create a PDF proofer for backup.

Closer Look: KDP Print Previewer
The Print Previewer from Amazon KDP allows a flip through exercise similar to a "Look Inside" feature on the Amazon published page. It gives warnings on format issues, images outside of the page size, page sequencing errors and endnote sequencing errors. In most cases, the Print Previewer errors, like photo quality, can be overridden to get the book published.

BOOK CONSTRUCTION ZONE

There is a B&W paperback and color paperback option for ordering. For the B&W paperback book, the cover page shown is in color, the internal content also shows in color on the screen, yet it will be printed in B&W.

Amazon KDP Print Previewer: Example 1
Upload print ready interior (PDF) into Amazon software

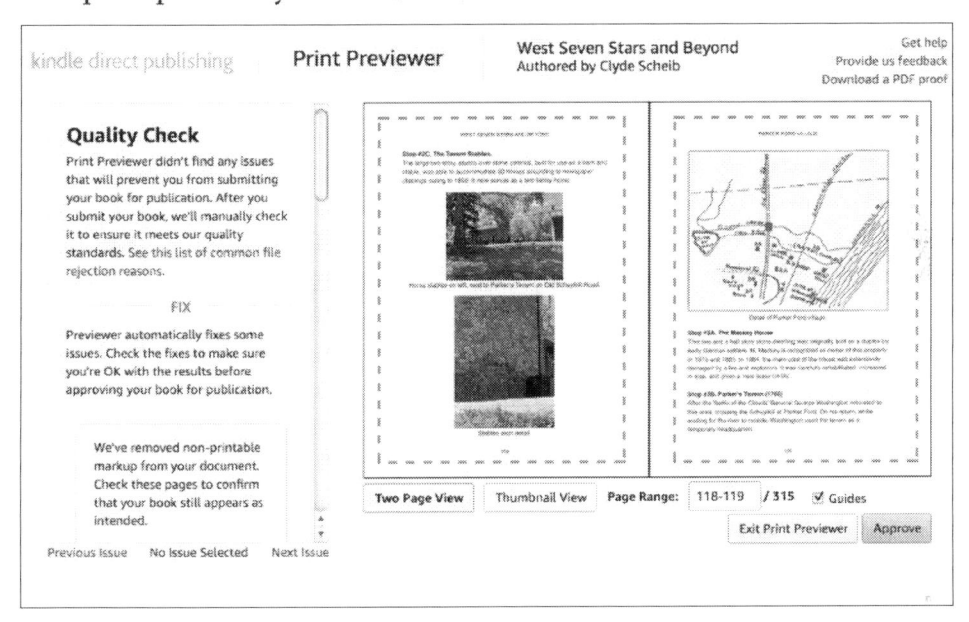

Closer Look: KDP Print Previewer Internal Content
The Print Previewer is now used on the base content with a two page view. The dotted guide lines are where the text should remain within. A quality check automatically fixes minor issues.

Other issues up to the Editor:

1. Resolve metadata issues. Check information in the manuscript and cover files match the book details (e.g., title, author name, edition, language, ISBN, etc.) entered during title setup.

Amazon KDP Print Previewer: Example 2

Upload print ready interior (PDF) into Amazon software

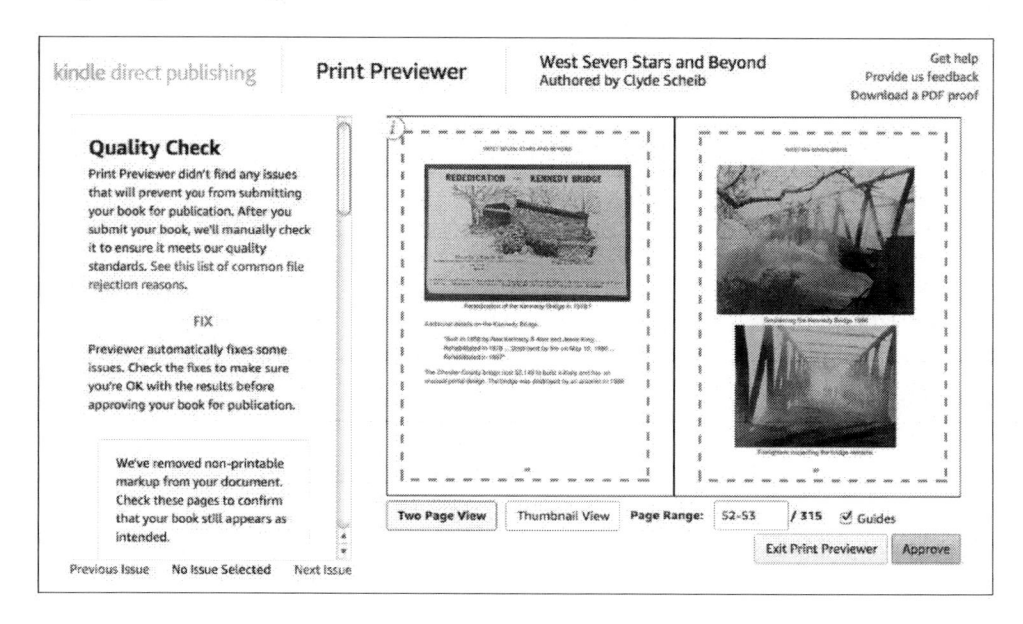

2. Resolve cover and spine text issues. Check to prevent spine text from wrapping onto the front or back cover. Make sure the text is completely inside the guides. Books need at least 100 pages to have spine text. Text is at least a 7-point font.

3. Resolve bleed issues. To prevent text from getting cut off during manufacturing, make sure it's completely inside the guides. If content (e.g., images) is supposed to extend to the edge of the page, make sure there are no white gaps.

Amazon KDP Print Previewer: Example 3

Upload print ready interior (PDF) into Amazon software

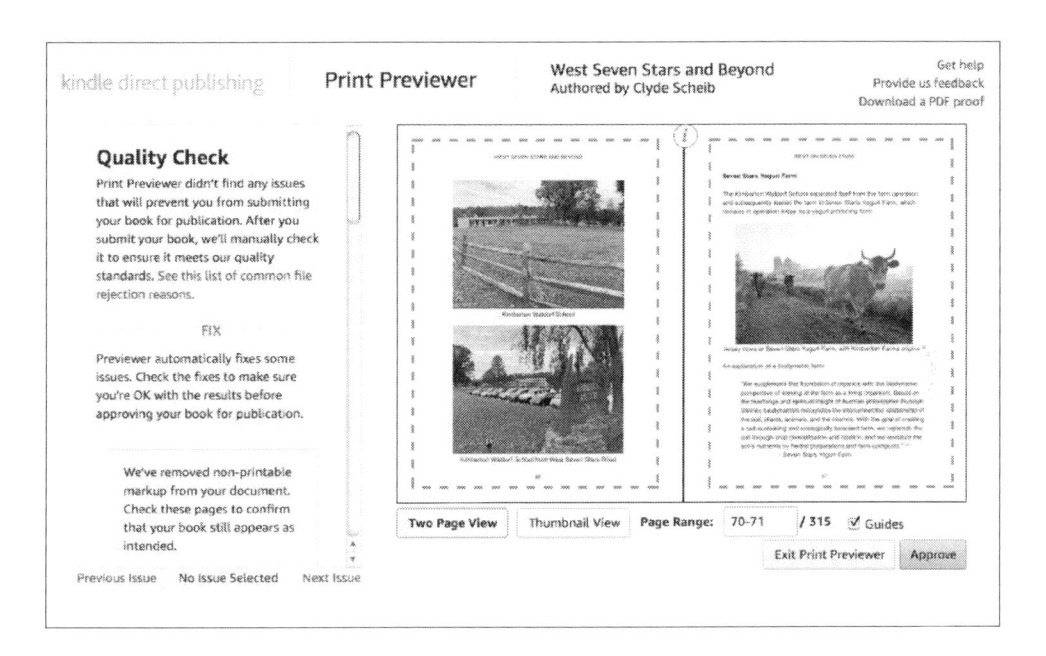

4. Resolve template issues. If a template was used, make sure to customize or remove all placeholder text (e.g., table of contents, headers, footers). Check all parts of the book, including:
   - Title page
   - Copyright page
   - Headers and footers
   - Front and back cover
   - Spine

5. Margins. Check manuscript content doesn't extends past the margins. This can cause the content from getting cut off during manufacturing. The text on the cover shouldn't extend past the cover edge. This can cause the text to be cut off during manufacturing.

Amazon KDP Print Previewer: Page View

- Check page overrun, format, page sequencing
- Check image quality, endnote sequencing

KDP Print Previewer: Page View
The thumbnail view or multiple pages view on Amazon's KDP Print Previewer shows page breaks, photo alignment, and page numbering for editing purposes.

1. Resolve pagination/blank pages issues. Check the page numbers in the manuscript file are in sequential order. There should be no more than two consecutive blank pages at the beginning or middle of the manuscript file and/or 10 consecutive blank pages at the end.

Order Hard Copy Proofs

Author Clyde Scheib with proof copies including an experimental cover. Once final proof is acceptable by Author and Editor, it's time to publish.

Order Hard Copy Proofs
The Author is holding several proof or sample copies of the book, and the final published book to the far right. A proof allows the Author and Editor to see a draft of the book in it's final form. It was through this review and proof editing process that an acceptable interior and preferred cover of the book was determined.

Publish the Book - Summary
Once the hardcopy proof is acceptable to the Author, the Editor submits the book for publishing. Amazon employees review the book, and if acceptable to their guidelines, the book is formally published to the main Amazon.com web site.

Next the Editor moves off the KDP software and to the Amazon.com web site, which is the public facing of how the book is displayed, described and ordered. The remainder of this section is configuring the Amazon.com web site.

The Amazon Published Page

- Print On Demand (POD) technology
- Storyline description is recap of contents
- "Follow the Author" links to Author page
- "Look Inside" feature is active (vs disabled)

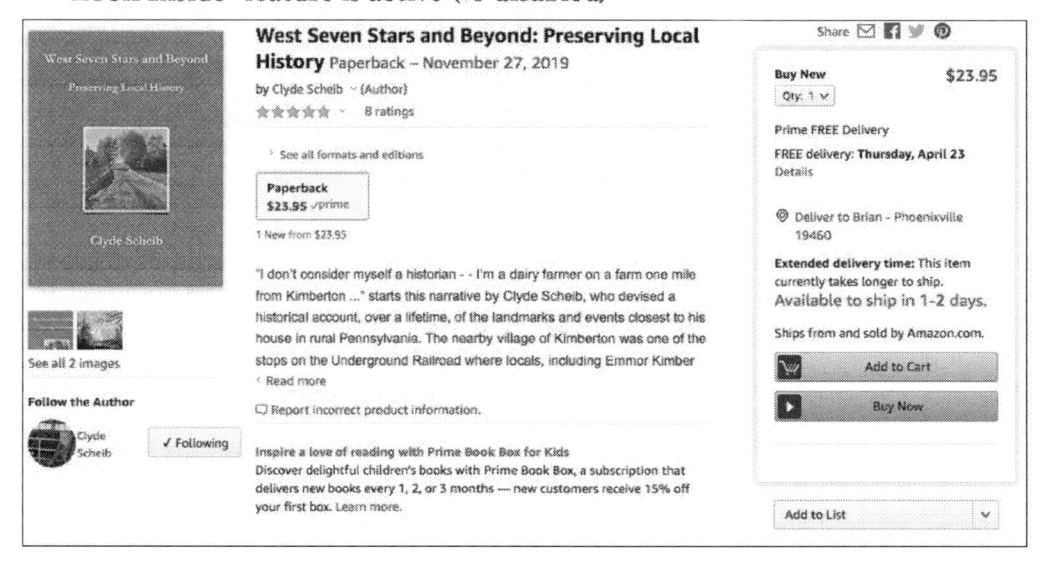

The Amazon Published Page - Public View
As mentioned, the Print On Demand (POD) technology means each book is printed once an order is placed. Under the previous practice, a book would be created in bulk, say 1000 copies printed and the purchaser would receive, for example, number 565 of the available copies. This leaves the distribution of the book up to the Author/Editor. In the POD model, Amazon handles the order taking through distribution, making it easier to distribute.

The description shares the books storyline or introduction to the reader. The "Look Inside" feature is activated automatically with each published book and shows the table of contents and a set percent of the books inner content. You can request this feature be disabled with a call to Amazon KDP. In this case study the product description was lengthened and the "Look Inside" feature was disabled.

BOOK CONSTRUCTION ZONE

The Amazon Published Page (cont'd)

Click to read full description ...

The Amazon Published Page (cont'd)

The Amazon published page has a description overview, book formats, edition options, a link to the Authors Page and a link to Follow the Author.

The reader can follow this part of the case study by searching on Amazon.com website using terms: "Clyde Scheib" or "West Seven Stars and Beyond".

The Amazon Published Page - Detail

The Amazon Published Page - Detail
The Description detail on the Amazon published page:

> "I don't consider myself a historian - - I'm a dairy farmer on a farm one mile from Kimberton ..." starts this narrative by Clyde Scheib, who devised a historical account, over a lifetime, of the landmarks and events closest to his house in rural Pennsylvania. The nearby village of Kimberton was one of the stops on the Underground Railroad where locals, including Emmor Kimber and John Vickers, shielded fugitive slaves on the road to the north. In the center of the village is the 18th century Kimberton Inn (1796) and the Sign of the Bear Tavern that has sheltered drovers and stage coach passengers along their travels. George Washington's troops marched through the village in 1777 after the Battle of the Brandywine.

Looking out his window and across a field, the Author sees remnants of the Sowbelly Railroad, a nickname for the DL&R line, that struggled to aid industrial growth in the mid to late 1800's.

Taking center stage of this historical narrative is a single road, West Seven Stars, where the Author has lived his entire life. The Kennedy Covered Bridge (1856) has provided passage over the French Creek for over 150 years and has survived man's intrusions. Next to the bridge is the Rudolf Steiner influenced Kimberton Farms, which became the Kimberton Waldorf School. The biodynamic Seven Stars Yogurt Farm and historian Estelle Cremers farm near the historic Seven Stars Inn (1754) completes "the end of the road."

Close by is the historic Parker Ford village that thrived with the Gerard Canal segment of the Schuylkill River Canal. Horse drawn boats pulled next to the canal on a towpath, with locks allowing boats to pass to another level and aqueducts crossing creeks; all part of the transportation revolution between 1815 -1890. Travelers stopped at Parker's Tavern (1766) to rest, either off a boat on the canal or a horse and wagon en-route to Philadelphia. At Parker Ford, George Washington lead the Continental Army across the Schuylkill River in the fight against the British (1777).

Down the road, the Author attended Hickory Grove one room schoolhouse, where the teacher taught all grades and boarded with the families during the school year. The Scheib Genealogy shows the family lineage and connections with Brownback and Swinehart families; all with long local lineages. Also, the Scheib Genealogy shows the German ancestral village and Swiss heritage. The creation of the nearby Revolutionary Soldiers Cemetery was a preservation effort to the memory of twenty-two fallen soldiers in the Revolutionary War, spearheaded by the Author.

The presentation of these storylines in close proximity to his house, shows Clyde Scheib's approach to preserving local history in rural Chester County, Pennsylvania.

This book, ISBN: 9798615410680 is the color version. A separate book, ISBN: 9781706215431 is the black and white version.

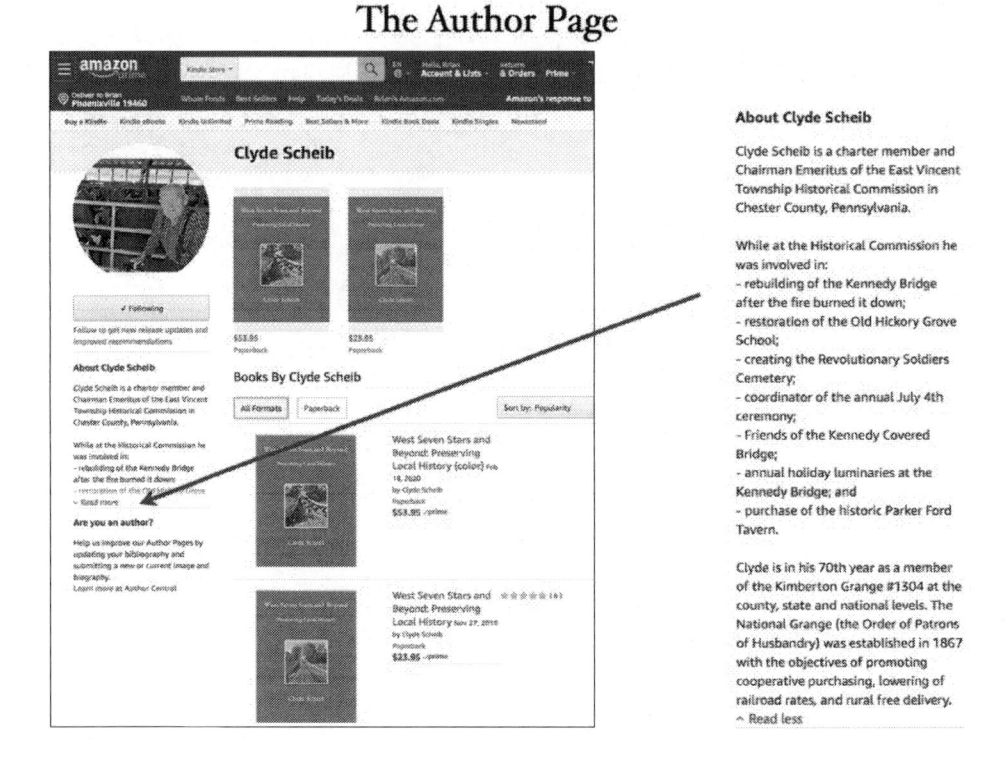

The Author Page - Public View

The "Author Page" gives the Author background and gathers multiple books by the author or versions of a single book, into one place. (Note: the biography content was taken from the latest book's Appendix section, called "Community Activities of Author" verbatim).

The Authors Page can be shared individually like a web site, since it has it's own URL. In this case the Author's URL is:

        amazon.com/author/clydescheib

This URL can be placed on Facebook, Twitter or an email to share with family, friends and followers.

Facebook Integration

This post on Facebook is generated from the Amazon.com website and has a direct link to the Authors page:

AMAZON.COM
Clyde Scheib
Follow Clyde Scheib and explore their bibliography from Amazon.com's Clyde Scheib Author Page.

Twitter Integration

This tweet on Twitter also is also generated from the amazon.com website and has link to the Authors page:

Check out my author page at this easy to remember url! amazon.com/author/clydescheib via @amazon

Pinterest and email integration from the Amazon.com website are also supported.

Author Central - Private View

This is the private working site for all updates to Author Central by the Editor/Author. It includes updates like add a new book, latest bibliography and scheduled presentation events. It's possible to "follow" the Author as new information becomes available.

In Author Central, the Author Page is similar to the public Author Page, except the books are listed separately under the tab "Books".

Author Central

BOOK CONSTRUCTION ZONE

Author Central Customer Reviews Summary

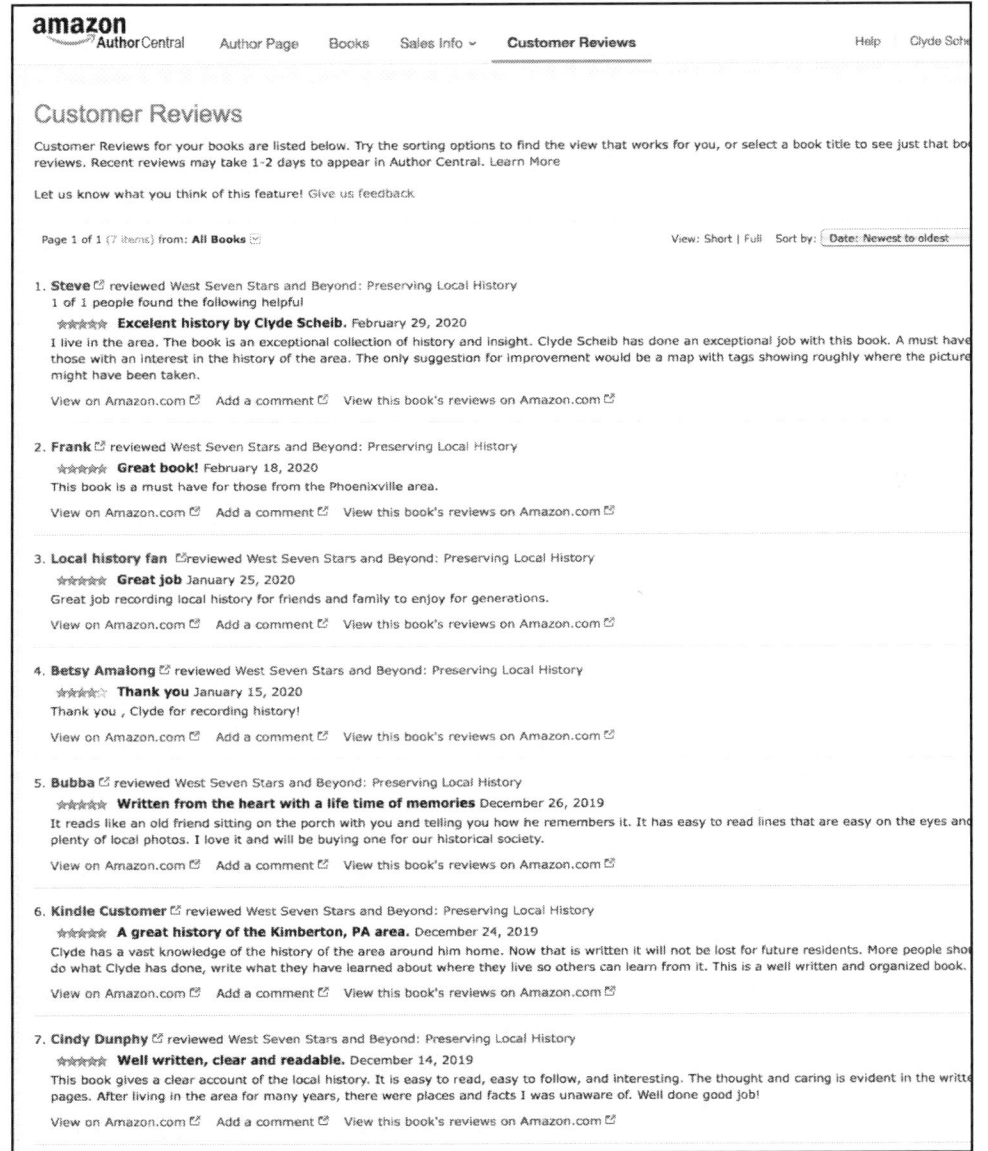

Customer Reviews

Customer Reviews for your books are listed below. Try the sorting options to find the view that works for you, or select a book title to see just that book's reviews. Recent reviews may take 1-2 days to appear in Author Central. Learn More

Let us know what you think of this feature! Give us feedback

Page 1 of 1 (7 items) from: All Books   View: Short | Full   Sort by: Date: Newest to oldest

1. **Steve** reviewed West Seven Stars and Beyond: Preserving Local History
   1 of 1 people found the following helpful
   ★★★★★ **Excelent history by Clyde Scheib.** February 29, 2020
   I live in the area. The book is an exceptional collection of history and insight. Clyde Scheib has done an exceptional job with this book. A must have those with an interest in the history of the area. The only suggestion for improvement would be a map with tags showing roughly where the pictures might have been taken.

2. **Frank** reviewed West Seven Stars and Beyond: Preserving Local History
   ★★★★★ **Great book!** February 18, 2020
   This book is a must have for those from the Phoenixville area.

3. **Local history fan** reviewed West Seven Stars and Beyond: Preserving Local History
   ★★★★★ **Great job** January 25, 2020
   Great job recording local history for friends and family to enjoy for generations.

4. **Betsy Amalong** reviewed West Seven Stars and Beyond: Preserving Local History
   ★★★★☆ **Thank you** January 15, 2020
   Thank you, Clyde for recording history!

5. **Bubba** reviewed West Seven Stars and Beyond: Preserving Local History
   ★★★★★ **Written from the heart with a life time of memories** December 26, 2019
   It reads like an old friend sitting on the porch with you and telling you how he remembers it. It has easy to read lines that are easy on the eyes and plenty of local photos. I love it and will be buying one for our historical society.

6. **Kindle Customer** reviewed West Seven Stars and Beyond: Preserving Local History
   ★★★★★ **A great history of the Kimberton, PA area.** December 24, 2019
   Clyde has a vast knowledge of the history of the area around him home. Now that is written it will not be lost for future residents. More people should do what Clyde has done, write what they have learned about where they live so others can learn from it. This is a well written and organized book.

7. **Cindy Dunphy** reviewed West Seven Stars and Beyond: Preserving Local History
   ★★★★★ **Well written, clear and readable.** December 14, 2019
   This book gives a clear account of the local history. It is easy to read, easy to follow, and interesting. The thought and caring is evident in the written pages. After living in the area for many years, there were places and facts I was unaware of. Well done good job!

Customer Reviews are key to promoting the book and Author. The results of marketing efforts and getting the book circulated in the community become evident here.

Author Central Book Editorial Reviews

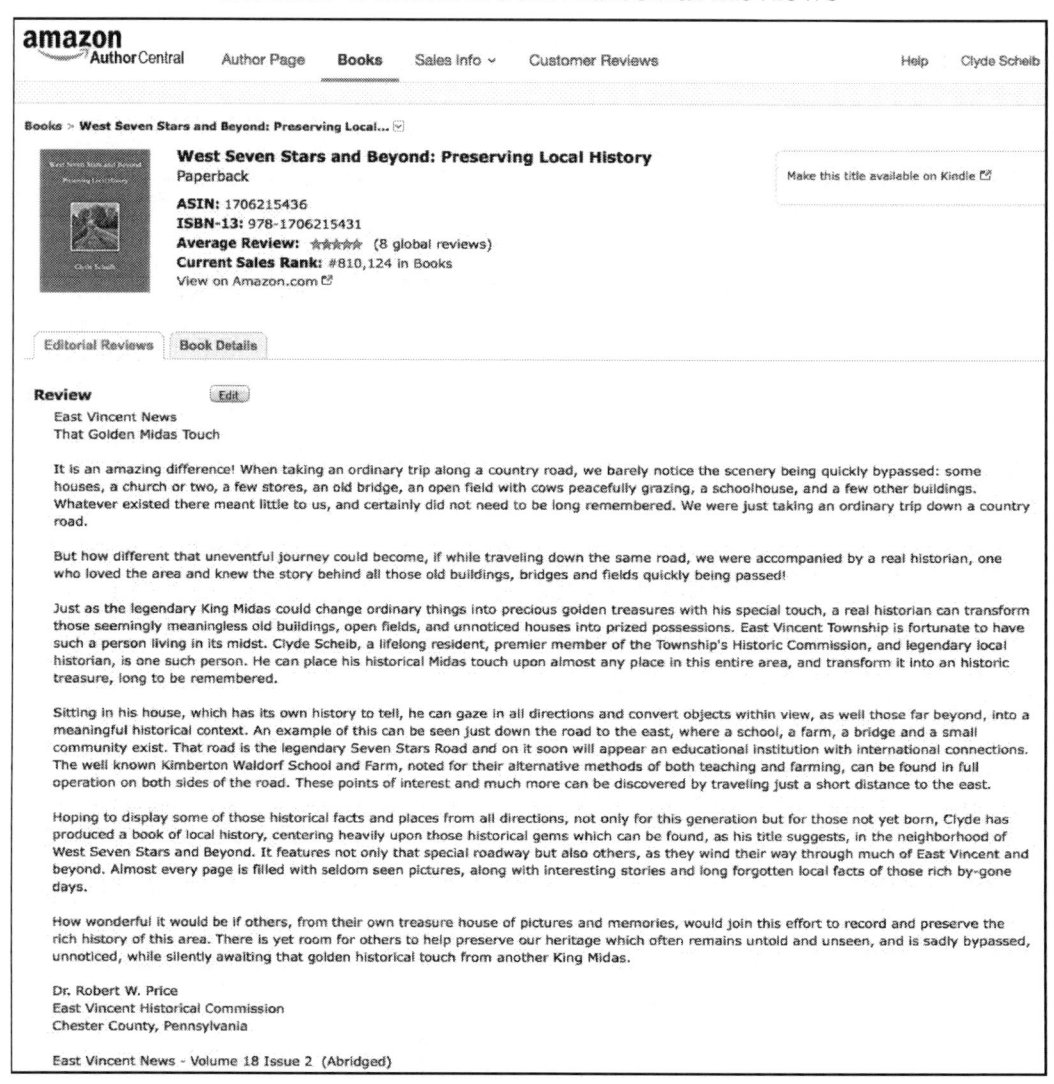

Books > West Seven Stars and Beyond: Preserving Local...

West Seven Stars and Beyond: Preserving Local History
Paperback

ASIN: 1706215436
ISBN-13: 978-1706215431
Average Review: ★★★★★ (8 global reviews)
Current Sales Rank: #810,124 in Books
View on Amazon.com

Make this title available on Kindle

Editorial Reviews | Book Details

Review [Edit]

East Vincent News
That Golden Midas Touch

It is an amazing difference! When taking an ordinary trip along a country road, we barely notice the scenery being quickly bypassed: some houses, a church or two, a few stores, an old bridge, an open field with cows peacefully grazing, a schoolhouse, and a few other buildings. Whatever existed there meant little to us, and certainly did not need to be long remembered. We were just taking an ordinary trip down a country road.

But how different that uneventful journey could become, if while traveling down the same road, we were accompanied by a real historian, one who loved the area and knew the story behind all those old buildings, bridges and fields quickly being passed!

Just as the legendary King Midas could change ordinary things into precious golden treasures with his special touch, a real historian can transform those seemingly meaningless old buildings, open fields, and unnoticed houses into prized possessions. East Vincent Township is fortunate to have such a person living in its midst. Clyde Scheib, a lifelong resident, premier member of the Township's Historic Commission, and legendary local historian, is one such person. He can place his historical Midas touch upon almost any place in this entire area, and transform it into an historic treasure, long to be remembered.

Sitting in his house, which has its own history to tell, he can gaze in all directions and convert objects within view, as well those far beyond, into a meaningful historical context. An example of this can be seen just down the road to the east, where a school, a farm, a bridge and a small community exist. That road is the legendary Seven Stars Road and on it soon will appear an educational institution with international connections. The well known Kimberton Waldorf School and Farm, noted for their alternative methods of both teaching and farming, can be found in full operation on both sides of the road. These points of interest and much more can be discovered by traveling just a short distance to the east.

Hoping to display some of those historical facts and places from all directions, not only for this generation but for those not yet born, Clyde has produced a book of local history, centering heavily upon those historical gems which can be found, as his title suggests, in the neighborhood of West Seven Stars and Beyond. It features not only that special roadway but also others, as they wind their way through much of East Vincent and beyond. Almost every page is filled with seldom seen pictures, along with interesting stories and long forgotten local facts of those rich by-gone days.

How wonderful it would be if others, from their own treasure house of pictures and memories, would join this effort to record and preserve the rich history of this area. There is yet room for others to help preserve our heritage which often remains untold and unseen, and is sadly bypassed, unnoticed, while silently awaiting that golden historical touch from another King Midas.

Dr. Robert W. Price
East Vincent Historical Commission
Chester County, Pennsylvania

East Vincent News - Volume 18 Issue 2 (Abridged)

This is a private view of Book Editorial Reviews usually written from experts within a genre. In this case study, the Editorial Review was taken from the East Vincent News, a quarterly newsletter to 7,000 plus residents living in East Vincent Township, Chester County, Pennsylvania. It was written by Dr. Robert W. Price of the East Vincent Township Historical Commission. It was placed on Author Central Editorial Review in an abridged format because it exceeded Amazon's upper word limit.

Chapter 3. Marketing Local History

It is amazing what you can accomplish if you do not care who gets the credit. - Harry S. Truman

Share

Share

The Author and Editor begin the process of marketing the published local history book. "Share" is promoting the finished product and getting it in circulation in the community.

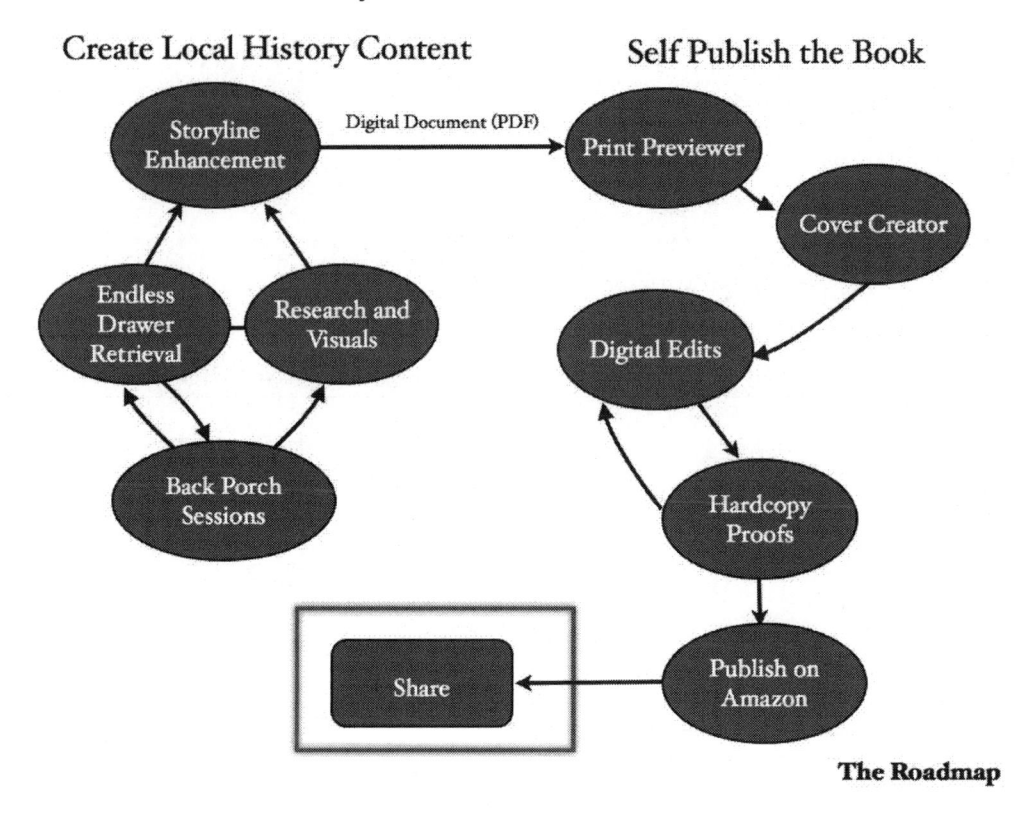

Create Local History Content / Self Publish the Book

- Storyline Enhancement
- Endless Drawer Retrieval
- Research and Visuals
- Back Porch Sessions
- Digital Document (PDF) → Print Previewer
- Cover Creator
- Digital Edits
- Hardcopy Proofs
- Publish on Amazon
- **Share**

The Roadmap

Share / The Roadmap

Having created the book on KDP and published the book on Amazon.com, the roadmap turns to the "Share" or marketing process. As mentioned, the goal is to preserve local history and using the Amazon platform will guarantee the book is available for years to come. The core book could also be converted into an ebook or audiobook (ACX).

Share — Letting Others Know

- Email blasts to relatives, friends, locals
- Notify Township/ County Historical Commissions and Societies
- Present at Township Historical Commissions/ Societies
- Recorded webinars (Loom software)
- Distribute posters (ie Whole Foods bulletin boards)
- Share homemade "business" cards
- Post on Facebook Pages / Groups
- Notify libraries/Book request

Homemade Promotion Cards   Book Promotion Flyer

Share / Letting Others Know

Relatives and friends are the first to be notified of the books listing on Amazon. Next, local township historical commissions, area historical societies, libraries and bookstores are notified. The Author shares with fellow members of The Theodore Burr Covered Bridge Society and The Grange Society. Some of these organizations were part of the initial discovery process. Also, landmark businesses on West Seven Stars Road, a core theme of the book, were interested in seeing their organization described in a published local book. Those residents living in the area of the history storylines often appreciate being notified as well.

A book review in a township newsletter is another way to get a book known to the general public. Even better is a book review in a genre newsletter, like a regional Historic Network.

One simple method is to create homemade "business" cards with the book cover photo and Amazon ordering details. These cards can be circulated to acquaintances, at organizational meetings or posted on bulletin boards. Creating and distributing a poster sized flier can be placed on store bulletin boards, like a Whole Foods bulletin board.

Creating a broadcast email with a link to the book to recipients as a blind-cc (bcc) is effective. An email broadcast in this way prevents a long list of who was sent the email, which is a distraction for most recipients.

Presentations are a good way to share, especially to local historical commissions and society organizations. Library book readings of select chapter(s) can be informative and a way to get the book into the community. Recording a presentation in a webinar can be timely when an in-person presentation is not possible, like during pandemics. Recording software like Loom is effective for recording a slide presentation.

Sharing publishing news with a link to the Amazon book can be included in Facebook posts, both personal and business. Becoming a member of a Facebook group, both open or closed groups, can let others with similar interests view the book release. Members of a Facebook Group can post directly to the Group, whereas Facebook "Pages" restrict followers from posting directly on the page, requiring an administrator to post. One can always request the administrator to make the post. Twitter and Instagram are other social media platforms to share the book.

Connecting with libraries and universities in cities near where landmarks are located is also effective. Depending on the library policy, formally request the library obtain the title, or as an alternative, donate the book to the library.

Creating an Author blog on the Wordpress platform is a method to update followers. This augments the Amazon Author Page and can be more interactive to share current projects or create local history posts related to the book chapters.

One can measure web analytics on the website/blog, Facebook likes, retweets or likes on Twitter and KDP Reports from authorized purchases. Twitter and Facebook can drive people to the blog and vice versa. The goal is to get the word out and preserve local history.

Distribution Channels

- Amazon Standard Channel: USA

- Amazon Expanded Channels: Canada, Europe (FR, UK, Italy, Spain, DE)

- Manual Distribution
- Libraries (county level)
- Libraries (local level)
- Township Historical Commissions
- Historical Societies
- Bookstores

ie. Chester County Library System
ie. East Vincent Township Historical Commission
ie. Chester County Historical Society (CCHS)
ie. Spring-Ford Area Historical Society
ie. Independent Bookstores in area

Distribution Channels
The Amazon Distribution Channels are grouped by Standard Channels and Expanded Channels including European countries and Canada. Libraries and bookstores are at the expanded channel. Certain trim sizes are not eligible for expanded channels. The Amazon Distribution Channels are at no additional cost.

About the Author:
Clyde Scheib has lived 80 plus years on the same street and has collected a lifetime of history. A dairy farmer by background, Clyde is a local historian well recognized in historical societies and commissions in Chester County, PA. Clyde's approach to preserving local history came to fruition when his writings were officially published. The book is called *West Seven Stars and Beyond: Preserving Local History* by Clyde Scheib. It is available in black and white (ISBN: 978-1706215431) and color (ISBN: 979-8615410680).

About the Editor:
Brian Wilde has an interest in keeping local history stories alive. Brian was fortunate to hear firsthand stories from his neighbor Clyde Scheib, who kept scrupulous notes on the Pennsylvania heritage surrounding him. Applying his technical management background, (BS Engineering, University at Buffalo SUNY), Brian teamed with Clyde to create and publish the local history book: *West Seven Stars and Beyond: Preserving Local History*. He lives in East Vincent Township, Chester County, Pennsylvania.

Clyde Scheib with maps he created.

Author Comments

The Author made the following comments on publishing *West Seven Stars and Beyond: Preserving Local History*:

"We had a lot of fun creating this book!"

"I couldn't have done this book without the Editor."

"This is one of my biggest accomplishments in my retirement years."

Editor Comments

"The Editor's role is to **listen** to the Author and put his storylines first supported by research and the latest publishing and marketing technologies. Conducting historical **research** is a give and take; gathering online materials, visiting historical libraries and landmarks always coupled with the Authors knowledge and bolstered by materials from the "endless drawer". As an **enabler**, the local history book, *West Seven Stars and Beyond,* was created and published with digital tools and shared with the community. Seeing the Author's reaction to his publishing achievement and community accolades is priceless."

Leaving Tips

> I don't publish anything I haven't worked over 100 times. - Donald Hall

Tips on Self Publishing a Local History Book From Editor Viewpoint

- Scheduled reviews with Author
- Create self imposed deadlines
- Utilize self publishing vendor support
- Focus on the end result: The Book
- Listen, learn and have fun
- Keep running tally of endnote citations
- Compliment images with text
- Leverage research tools
- Accept low quality historical images
- Order a hard copy "proof" for review
- Keep The Author informed
- Engage subject matter experts
- Build on municipal government studies
- Use best of breed software vendors

Editor's role: "take what author tosses your way and make it readable and presentable".
- BW

Tips on Self Publishing a Local History Book From Editor Viewpoint

1. Scheduled reviews with the Author
   Using sound project management techniques will assure the project moves forward at a steady pace. For example, setting up weekly

reviews at predefined times with the Author at a mutually comfortable location keeps the project on track. (back porch sessions)

2. Create self imposed deadlines
Milestone timelines should be thought out and planned, milestones like; complete content research, create vendor account, perform digital edits, obtain hard copy proofs and publish on Amazon.

3. Utilize self publishing vendor support
As issues arise, utilize the call center support from the self publishing vendors; in this case Lulu and Amazon KDP. Many of these vendors have knowledgeable and courteous self publishing experts available to give guidance.

4. Focus on the end result: The Book
Research is a key component to creating content, but can easily get the team sidetracked with nice to know information and increase the time to get the book published. If research is not focused on adding value to the book or for direct inclusion in the book, it should be either shelved or at a minimum be given a lower priority.

5. Listen, learn and have fun
Most local history projects are a compilation of research and the Author's views on the history. Some efforts never get completed, nor published, if that is the end goal. Having an Editor that listens and learns from the Author and at the same time both create an element of excitement and fun, makes the process enjoyable, challenging and worthwhile. Plus, getting the book published becomes a major event in the Author's life, especially if he/she are new to being published.

6. Capture sources
Keeping a running tally on sources, of the photos and/or text, makes the creation of the endnotes section much easier than a one time end of the book exercise that can be time consuming. The Apple "pages" word processing program has a endnote feature that keeps track of the endnote number that is automatically reordered as new endnotes are documented. That is a real time saver.

7. Compliment images with text
   Positioning images with related text makes the book interesting and easy to read and follow.

8. Leverage research tools
   The Author's research tools can be other historians, book collections, societies and knowledge acquired over the years. The Editor performs internet research, museum and landmark visits. Sites like Livable Places are of value. Technology tools at the County Public Library include high speed multiple feed scanners that efficiently generate digital text from hard copy documents. Extensive oral history catalogues can be found at the library. Several other sources are the Ancestry.com website and the Find-A-Grave website for genealogy research. History from the organizations under study, for example in this case study, The Kimberton Waldorf School and Seven Stars Inn both had their history documented on-line.

9. Photo of a photo
   Using an iPhone, camera or other smartphone, take a photo of a photo for efficient and quick results. Record the citation of the source photo for inclusion in the endnotes.

10. Accept low quality historical images
    Consider photo quality as a secondary consideration since vintage images do not get better with higher resolution. Many technologists want the ultimate photo quality, when in realty, an image that gets the message across is a better utilization of time.

11. Order a hard copy "proof" for review
    Order the optional hard copy paperback Proof for review. Once errors are noticed and corrected, ordering another proof is a best practice. Notice proofs are optional, so you can go right to publish, if desired and under a time constraint.

12. Keep The Author informed
    Keeping the Author informed with status updates and sharing research breakthroughs brings the chemistry required to move the project forward.

13. Engage subject matter experts
    Subject matter experts can be varied; librarians, genealogy and history consultants, self publishing vendor support and social media experts. Librarians including specialists like archivists at the Chester County Historical Society are great resources. Getting a genealogy consultant involved could yield ancestral knowledge that would otherwise be left unearthed for several more generations.

14. Build on municipal government studies
    The Editor was a participant in a multi township Historic Park Conceptual Plan which jumped started the "Parker Ford Village" chapter. Past studies can prove valuable for historical explanations, like the Master Plan for the Parkerford Tavern and the original historical nomination document from the National Register of Historic Places.

15. Use best of breed software vendors
    Use best of breed software vendors, like Lulu for the cover Creator and Amazon for the Publishing platform. Create interplay between vendor tools. An example is Lulu's Cover Creator PDF output file as the input to Amazon KDP software.

16. Create an Author's page
    Create on Amazon's Author Central background of the author, editorial reviews and a list of current books.

17. Engage social media influencers
    The benefit of social media influencers is they are well known in the niche historical circles and can assist in getting the book into their followers.

18. Promote book reviews
    Nudge friends to be active creating a book review on Amazon. Note: a book review on Amazon can only be written by verified purchasers.

19. Update manuscript after published
    Manuscript changes, if minor, can be deployed to the same edition and is invisible to the end customer. Significant changes (over 10%) is a considered a new edition and requires publishing as a new book.

Appendix

> We learn to do something by doing it. There is no other way. - John Holt

What is a Local History Virtual Workshop?

- "Create" Session by Unpacking Memories

- Publish in the Construction Zone

- "Share" by Marketing to the Community

- Launch the Marketing Effort

Local History Virtual Workshop
The virtual workshop utilizes techniques written in this Case Study guide book that enables others to write content and publish their own local history book. It is conducted remotely.

This is an outline for a local history virtual workshop:

"Create" Sessions
- conduct a walking tour of a neighborhood street or village
- create a local history storyline
- conduct an ancestor search on Ancestry.com and "Find a Grave" site
- create a genealogy lineage chart
- find a topic in a historic newspaper article
- use an existing oral history or conduct an oral history, modified to a book format
- access Chester County resources (like the Futhey / Cope book) for photos and storylines
- identify landmarks nearby your residence; research these landmarks
- create a draft of "My Local History" PDF document to test

"*Wonder*", Pen & Ink, by Lisa Kagan

APPENDIX

Make a Proof Book
- make cover in Lulu or KDP software
- set up Amazon KDP site
- create book template and import core document
- order proof copy
- continue set up on Amazon; cost, description, "Authors Page"
- publish on Amazon.com

"Share" Session
- activate a social media platform
- create a "business" card
- create a poster
- create a broadcast email

The Mill at Anselma in Chester Springs PA, built 1747

HOW TO WRITE AND PUBLISH A LOCAL HISTORY BOOK

Final Product

- Share the proof book
- Present a slide show to friends utilizing the output from the workshop

Final word: The virtual workshop can be the start to creating and publishing a local history book that will be available in the community for many years to come.

"*Release*", Mixed Media, by Lisa Kagan

Acknowledgments

The Editor along with the Author express gratitude to Alda Scheib whose diligence, strategic inputs and knowledge of local history added immense value to this effort. Alda was the source of many ideas and suggestions to gather the research needed to move the project to completion.

Made in the USA
Columbia, SC
21 July 2020